TOP·TEN

VALERIE WILDING

Illustrated by **Michael Tickner**

Hippo

For Kieran, with love.

Scholastic Children's Books,
Commonwealth House, 1-19 New Oxford Street,
London WC1A 1NU, UK

A division of Scholastic Limited
London ~ New York ~ Toronto ~ Sydney ~ Auckland
Mexico City ~ New Delhi ~ Hong Kong

Published in the UK by Scholastic Ltd, 2000

ISBN 0 439 99622 8

Typeset by Falcon Oast Graphic Art, East Hoathly, East Sussex.
Printed by Cox & Wyman, Reading, Berks

2 4 6 8 10 9 7 5 3 1

Dickens Stories

Contents

Introduction

Open a novel by Charles Dickens and you might...
- slink along a narrow alleyway that never sees the sun to visit the darkest, dirtiest, stinking hovels of Victorian London.
- attend lessons in a school where badly-treated pupils learn to cope with cruel, ignorant teachers.
- learn what it's like to pick a pocket.
- discover how easy it is to find yourself in jail.

One minute you'll be giggling and the next you'll be sniffling quietly as the plot twists and turns.

Of one thing you can be sure – you're never alone with a Dickens story. Open the book and you open the door to a crowd of characters who leap into life from the page. Mr Dickens created over two thousand of them.

In his world, you'll find murderers and madmen, crooks and conmen, beautiful young girls and wicked old hags, the kind and the cruel, the innocent and the guilty.

BUT these are big books. You can't whip through them while you're waiting for the school bus! One thing Victorians had plenty of was time, and that's what you need to read a Dickens story. It's time well spent. Your reward is free entry into the imagination of one of the greatest writers ever.

So, here are ten of his stories, told in shorter ways than the Victorians were used to – and very different ways. (I wonder if Queen Victoria would have been amused...)

Story 10: A Christmas Carol

Mr Dickens was already famous when he wrote our number ten story, A Christmas Carol. If they'd had fan clubs in 1843, his would have been GIGANTIC.

He was so popular that a stonking great 6,000 copies sold on the FIRST DAY, and 2,000 more were ordered before the printers had a chance to catch their breath and produce more.

A Christmas Carol is the story of a nasty, mean-minded, mean-spirited old codger called Ebenezer Scrooge, who ended up…

Well, to find out how he ended up, let's go elsewhere. Let's go to the spirit world – not the local pub, but the world of ghoulies and ghosties, where a special meeting of the Haunting Action Group is in session.

The X~mas Files

Chief Spectre: Fellow HAGs, we're gathered here, together, all of us –

Old Croner: Get on with it. It's Christmas Eve. Some of us have got parties to go to.

Chief Spectre: OK. We're having this meeting because a fellow ghost wants to sort someone out. Jacob?

Jacob: My name's Jacob Marley. I've been dead seven years. When I was alive, my business partner was Ebenezer Scrooge – a miser – a hater of mankind. Scrooge is so stingy he won't even pay to have my name removed from the sign over our – or rather, his – office.

Ghosts: Shame.

Jacob: He is so mean, he gives his clerk, Bob Cratchit, only one day off a year – Christmas Day.

Ghosts: Rotter.

Jacob: He is *so* mean, Bob has to ask permission to put a single lump of coal on the fire in his freezing office.

Ghosts: Nasty.

Jacob: Today, a boy started to sing a Christmas carol through his keyhole. Guess what Scrooge did?

Gilbert de Goole: Gave him a mince pie?

Jacob: He chased him with a ruler.

Ghosts: He didn't!

Jacob: He did. And Scrooge told his dead sister's son –

Old Croner: His nephew.

Jacob: Thank you, I do know that. He told his nephew Fred who asked him to Christmas lunch, "Every idiot who goes about with 'Merry Christmas' on his lips should be boiled with his own pudding, and buried with a stake of holly through his heart."

Will Smallbone: Wooo!

Jacob: Bah!

Will Smallbone: Wooo bah?

Jacob: No. "Bah" is what Scrooge said when Fred wished him a Merry Christmas.

Ghosts: Bah to Scrooge! Bah! Bah! Bah! Bah!

Chief Spectre: Stop it. You're acting like sheep. Jacob, continue.

Jacob: When two jolly gents came to the door collecting for the poor and destitute, Scrooge asked,

"Are there no prisons? Workhouses?" The jolly gents explained that some of the poor couldn't go there, and many would rather die. And Scrooge said … he said…

Chief Spectre: Yes, Jacob? What did he say?

Jacob: He said, "If they would rather die, they had better do it!"

Ghosts: No-o-o-o!

Jacob: Now I admit that I wasn't always the nicest of people when I was alive. In fact, I was just the teeniest bit like Scrooge, but I know better now.

Old Croner: So what do you want from us?

Jacob: I want to show Scrooge how different life could be, if only he'd help others less fortunate than himself, and spread a little cheer.

Chief Spectre: I call upon Old Croner, Gilbert de Goole and Will Smallbone. Your mission, should you choose to accept it, is to help Jacob to change the character of Ebenezer "Bah" Scrooge.

Old Croner: I'll have a bash.

Gilbert de Goole: De Gooles never refuse a challenge.

Will Smallbone: Count me in.

Jacob: Thanks, guys.

Chief Spectre: Let me have your reports when you've finished.

Jacob Marley's Report

To welcome him home, I turned Scrooge's door knocker into an image of my face, all ghostly glow and staring eyes. Was he scared? Not on your life – er, death. He lit his candle, said, "Pooh, pooh," and slammed the door. The stairs were dark, but he didn't care. Darkness was cheap. Up he went.

My knocker-face did have some effect, because he checked carefully all round his nasty, mean little rooms, even under the bed. Of course, he couldn't see me, but I was waiting.

Oh yes, I was waiting.

Meanwhile, I turned all the pictures on his fireplace tiles into little portraits of me. Scrooge's reaction was, "Humbug!" He didn't believe in ghosts (not then, he didn't!) so I rang a few bells, softly at first, then louder. I stopped them suddenly, leaving a deathly silence. Next I headed for the cellar and started the clanking chain routine. I flung the cellar door open – boom! – and dragged the chains all the way up the stairs, closer and closer, until – get this – I passed straight through his door!

It worked. He nearly freaked out when I materialized in front of him.

I say it worked, but he wasn't totally convinced. "You don't believe in me," I moaned.

(His reply was extremely insulting, so please keep it confidential.) "I don't," he said. "You may be an undigested bit of beef, a crumb of cheese. There's more of gravy than of grave about you, whatever you are!"

I'll get you, I thought. I groaned and rattled, then warned him that three spirits would visit him at one o'clock in the morning. "You're lucky, Scrooge. You have a chance to change your wretched character," I wailed. "You don't want to end up like me, in chains for all eternity, do you?"

His face! Was he ever scared!

Tough, I thought, and went into reverse, out the window, a-moaning and a-wailing, and left it to Old Croner.

Old Croner's Report
Before I took over, I let my hair down – it's grown a lot since I was alive – and dressed in a white tunic, with a sparkly belt. I carried a sprig of holly and, for seasonal contrast, added a few summer flowers to the outfit. Gorgeous!

At this point, I'd like it placed on record that if Gilbert de Goole ever makes another remark about new clothes not doing much to improve an old face, I will personally vaporize him.

Anyway, I zipped into Scrooge's room as the church bell gonged once, and swooshed open the curtains round his mean little bed. I made a bright clear jet of light spring from my head, so he could see me.

"I am the Ghost of Christmas Past," I said. "Your past. I've come to remind you what it used to be like."

Once he'd calmed down, I whooshed things round a bit and showed him a time when he was a schoolboy. Everyone had gone home for Christmas, but Scrooge was left alone in the schoolroom. Looking on, he recalled his poor forgotten self and began to cry, so that was a good start. He blubbed about the boy who tried to sing a Christmas carol through his keyhole. "I should like to have given him something," he said.

I felt like pointing out that he'd tried to give the kid something – with a ruler.

He watched as I showed him another Christmas in the schoolroom, when he was older, but still alone and miserable. His sister rushed in. "I have come to bring you home, dear brother," she said.

This was cruel of me, because that sister died young. Not before she'd had a child, though: Scrooge's nephew, Fred – the one who invited him to Christmas dinner. Bet he wished he hadn't said, "Bah!"

Next, we shooshed to the warehouse where he'd been an apprentice to a dear old boy called Fezziwig. Inside, there was a whizzo party with feasting and dancing. "Yo ho, my boys!" Fezziwig cried. "No more work tonight." Scrooge cheered up when he remembered what fun he'd had there, but his expression soon changed.

"What's the matter?" I asked.

"I should like to be able to say a word or two to my clerk just now."

So! Remembering his boss's kindness had made Scrooge realize how rotten he was to Bob Cratchit. Good.

The next scenes made him miserable. He saw the girl he loved telling him money mattered more to him than she did. She broke off their engagement.

"Take me away!" Scrooge cried.

So I did. Back to his mean little bed. Hope that's OK.

16

Gilbert de Goole's Report

I set myself up in the next room to Scrooge. I made it look extremely grand and Christmassy, with decorations, a fire and a sort of throne for me — made of food! Pies and roast meats, puddings and sausages — it looked real enough to eat. "Come in, man," I called.

Scrooge's face! Old Croner must have done a great job, because he didn't give me any lip at all. He trembled violently, and didn't seem quite the tough old bird Jacob told us about.

"I am the Ghost of Christmas Present," I said. "You've never seen the like of me before."

He hadn't, either. With holly on my head, I looked good, even taller than I am in real life. Death, I mean.

I took him into the city streets. The church bells were ringing for Christmas Day, and people were going back and forth to bakers' shops with dishes of food. Yum — what memories!

We visited the home of Scrooge's clerk, Bob Cratchit. It was his one day off a year, and if I'd worked for Scrooge I wouldn't have been as cheerful as Bob. Talk about make the best of a bad job! The whole family had worked wonders with what they had, and were cheery and excited.

17

As we watched, Bob and his son walked in. At least, Bob walked, but he carried his little boy, Tiny Tim, on his shoulder. Tiny Tim had an iron frame on his poor leg, and held a crutch.

That family! They were something else! Happy, loving — everything Scrooge isn't. When dinner was over, Bob asked God to bless them all. Tiny Tim spoke up then. "God bless us, every one!" he said.

Scrooge was shaken. That little lad touched even his cold heart. "Spirit," said Scrooge, "tell me if Tiny Tim will live."

I went a bit mystic. "I see a vacant seat in the poor chimney corner, and a crutch without an owner."

"Oh, no, kind Spirit!" Scrooge cried. "Say he will be spared."

I had him now, so I put the boot in. "But if he's likely to die, then — he had better do it."

Good one, Gilbert, I thought. That's just what Scrooge himself had said about the poor and destitute. Let his words come back to haunt him.

He looked ashamed.

Well, tough turkey. He had it coming to him.

Next stop — Fred's house.

It shook Scrooge suddenly to find himself at his nephew's party — the one he'd refused to go to. It was a happy sight. The fire blazed brightly, and the family, who'd just finished dinner, chatted and laughed in the lamplight. You could have knocked me down with a quill pen when they drank a toast to their Uncle Scrooge.

"A merry Christmas to the old man, whatever he is," cried Fred.

I didn't let Scrooge stay to enjoy that.

Finally, I produced two starving, ragged children from beneath my robe.

"Spirit! Are they yours?" Scrooge asked.

"They are Man's," I said. "Their names are Ignorance and Want. Beware them both."

"Why? Haven't they anywhere to go? No one to care for them?" he cried.

Hah! Gotcha! "Are there no prisons?" I asked, using his own words again. "No workhouses?"

Masterstroke, eh? I couldn't top that, so I left.

Will Smallbone's Report

I appeared to Scrooge as the Ghost of Christmas Yet to Come. Like a mist creeping along the ground, I glided towards him, completely cloaked in deep black. No part of me was visible, except one bony hand which I

 stretched towards him.

As I loomed nearer, I could almost see the dread in his eyes.

"Spirit, are you going to show me the future?" Scrooge asked.

I didn't answer. That really spooked him, and as I moved away, he followed. He didn't dare not.

I showed him a group of men discussing someone they knew, who was dead. (Guess who.) They laughed and joked.

"It's likely to be a very cheap funeral," said one, "for upon my life I don't know of anybody to go to it."

I took Scrooge to a second-hand shop in the City slums, full of old rags, iron, bottles and bones. Some people came in carrying bundles of clothes, bed-curtains and so on, to sell. They laughed about how the owner wouldn't want them, now he was dead.

"He should have been kinder," one muttered. "If he had been, he'd have had somebody to look after him, instead of gasping out his last by himself."

Scrooge shuddered. "Spirit, that poor dead man could almost be me!"

(Thick, or what!)

"Show me," he begged, "someone who does have some feeling for a death."

I showed him a young mother. Her husband came in. He was a worried man, all right, but he couldn't disguise the delight in his voice.

"There is hope yet," he said. "He is dead."

The young mother's face lit up with relief. They talked of how they would now have time to pay their debts. The man they owed money to – the bully who would have ruined them – was out of their lives. Gone.

Scrooge was a trier, I'll give him that. Again he asked, "Let me see some tenderness connected with a death."

I took him to Bob Cratchit's. It would have upset anyone when the wife said, "Your father's late," and one of the children said, "I think he has walked a little slower than he used, these last few evenings."

The wife's voice broke as she said how Bob had walked very fast indeed with Tiny Tim upon his shoulder. "His father loved him so."

Bob arrived just then. He'd met Scrooge's nephew, Fred. "He told me," said Bob, "'If I can help you in any way, pray come to me.'"

Scrooge asked me who the dead man was. As we moved on, I let him look in his office window and see someone else in his place.

He was beginning to cotton on.

I liked this bit. Without saying a word, I took him to the churchyard, and pointed to a grave. Trembling, he crept towards the tombstone, and read: EBENEZER SCROOGE.

21

Oh boy! That did it!

"Spirit! Oh, no, no! Tell me I can change what you've shown me, by changing myself. I will honour Christmas in my heart," he promised, "and try to keep it all the year."

I got smaller and smaller, and changed into – his bedpost!

That was my job done, but Jacob was watching, so he'll tell you the outcome.

Jacob Marley's Report

When Scrooge saw his bed-curtains hadn't been sold to a second-hand shop, he was so happy he hugged them.

Shouting, "Merry Christmas!" as he dressed, he flung open the window to hear the church bells. He called down to a boy in the street, "What's today?"

"Today!" replied the boy. "Why, Christmas Day!"

"It's Christmas Day!" said Scrooge to himself. "I haven't missed it."

I couldn't believe what happened next. He ordered the biggest turkey he could get and had it sent to Bob Cratchit's.

He went out, wished everyone "Merry Christmas", and almost immediately met the jolly gents who'd been collecting for the poor. Scrooge whispered to them. It must have been something good, judging by their smiles.

Scrooge ended up at Fred's for lunch and had his best Christmas ever.

Next morning, I checked to make sure it hadn't been a one-day wonder, and found him up to one of his old tricks. He went to work early, just to catch Bob coming in late.

Bob sneaked in and tried to look as if he'd been there for ages, but Scrooge growled, "What do you mean by coming here at this time of day? I am not going to stand this sort of thing any longer. Therefore, I am about to raise your salary!"

And then he said, "I'll help your family, and especially Tiny Tim."

I nearly died. Oh. Well, you know what I mean.

MISSION ACCOMPLISHED

Rotten egg: Ebenezer Scrooge

"…a squeezing, wrenching, grasping, scraping, clutching, covetous old sinner! The cold within him froze his old features…"

Good egg: Tiny Tim

"…he hoped the people saw him in the church, because he was a cripple, and it might be pleasant to them to remember upon Christmas Day, who made lame beggars walk, and blind men see."

Top Facts 10: Dickens — the man

Mr Dickens left a wonderful legacy. His novels give a vivid picture of the nineteenth century as he knew it. Although the books were stuffed with imaginary characters, those characters reflected the men, women and children he listened to, watched and cared about — real people. Let's look at some facts about the man — Charles Dickens.

1 Getting "The Knowledge"

Charles Dickens was born in 1812, near Portsmouth, where his dad worked in the Navy pay office. The family moved to London when he was two, but then moved south again, to Chatham, in Kent. Charles was ten when they finally settled in London. Although he wasn't a true Londoner, he came to know the city as well as anyone. As an adult, he loved to walk the London streets. He walked by day and night — often covering eight or nine miles in the darkness. His books are stuffed with the characters and sights he saw and heard, the dirt, the smells — even the tastes! They truly give the flavour of Victorian London, the city that was his inspiration. One of Dickens's friends said, "…he sees and observes nine facts for any two that I see and observe."

2 Sticking to the job

When Charles was only twelve, his free-spending dad got into debt. Charles was sent to work in a warehouse, sticking labels on bottles of smelly boot-blacking for six or seven shillings (30–35p) a week. He loathed the building, the conditions and the stink but, to a writer, nothing is wasted. You can see how he used these experiences in *David Copperfield*: "I mingled my tears," says the hero, "with the water in which I was washing the bottles; and sobbed as if there were a flaw in my own

breast, and it were in danger of bursting." Eventually, Charles's dad was arrested and sent to Marshalsea debtors' prison. It was common in those days for the rest of the family to move in with a prisoner, so that's what the Dickens family did. Charles, who was twelve years old, could earn money, so he stayed outside, living alone in a rented room. Luckily his dad later inherited a little money, and Charles was able to leave the hated job.

3 Speed

Charles strove constantly to improve himself and to better his circumstances. At fifteen he worked as a solicitor's clerk, then became a freelance court reporter. With no recording equipment, reporters had to take notes by hand, so Charles taught himself shorthand in his spare time. He was soon so skilled that he became a Parliamentary reporter. "I had heard that many men distinguished in various pursuits had begun life by reporting the debates in Parliament," he wrote in *David Copperfield*. Before long, he was a reporter-on-the-move for the *Morning Chronicle*, often rewriting his shorthand notes in a carriage drawn by four horses, galloping at fifteen miles an hour! What would Charles have made of a laptop?

4 A bose by any other name

Charles John Huffam Dickens, being a rather remarkable man (a one-off, as they say), was known as

"The Inimitable". When he started his writing career, he had another name – one he'd selected himself: "Boz". His youngest brother, Augustus, was known as "Moses" and "Boses". (Perhaps it was Moses when Charles was fit and well, and Boses when he had a cold.) Boses was shortened to Boz and Charles liked it. He liked it so much that he gave the name to his eldest son, Charles Culliford Boz Dickens. Names were clearly important to Mr Dickens. Many of his characters have names that reflect their personalities. See if you can match the name to the description:

The characters

1. Wackford Squeers
2. Mrs Lupin
3. Toby Crackit
4. Charles Cheeryble
5. Charity Pecksniff

The descriptions

a) "A sturdy old fellow … with such a pleasant smile … and such a comical expression of … kindheartedness and good humour, lighting up his jolly old face." (*Nicholas Nickleby*)

b) "He had but one eye, and … a very sinister appearance, especially when he smiled, at which times his expression bordered closely on the villainous" (*Nicholas Nickleby*)

c) "…a landlady, with a face which bore testimony to her hearty participation in the good things of the larder and cellar… She was a widow, but years ago had passed through her state of weeds, and burst into flower again" (*Martin Chuzzlewit*)

d) Her "nose … was always very red at breakfast-time … it wore a scraped and frosty look, as if it had been rasped." (*Martin Chuzzlewit*)

e) A "flash" house-breaker, his hair was "tortured into long corkscrew curls, through which he occasionally thrust some very dirty fingers, ornamented with large, common rings." (*Oliver Twist*)

Answers: 1b), 2c), 3e), 4a), 5d).

5 The performance artist

Mr Dickens was theatre mad. As a boy he'd sung funny songs and recited poems in the local pub, and eventually became an amateur actor. He was so stage-struck that he fixed up an audition to become a professional. On the day, he had such a stinking cold that he decided to leave it until next season. However, he began to succeed as a journalist and gave up the idea of becoming a star. Just imagine, if he hadn't caught a cold, we might never have had his brilliant stories. (Who says viruses are all bad?) In the end Charles *did* become a performer, though not in the way he'd originally planned. He gave public readings from his books and, being the chap he was, he put his heart and soul into them. It's said that his reading of Nancy's murder in *Oliver Twist* was so terrifying that some women actually fainted. (A doctor once measured Dickens's own pulse before and after he read the bit about Nancy's murder, and found it had risen from about 80 to 124! Considering Dickens was standing still at a reading desk, he must have been pretty worked up!) Dickens often made his audience gasp – and laugh, too! Charles was like the hero

of his book, *Nicholas Nickleby*: "Nicholas personated a vast variety of characters … and attracted so many people to the theatre who had never been seen there before…"

6 Bird brain

Charles Dickens respected and loved animals. "The man as can form a ackerate judgment of a animal, can form a ackerate judgment of anythin'," says Sam Weller's dad in *The Pickwick Papers*. Dickens owned the usual cats and dogs, and even a pony, but his most unusual pet was Grip, the raven. Although Grip was a clever bird, he wasn't popular with everyone, as he bit children's ankles. He liked to bury cheese and coins in the garden  and was a good talker. Dickens loved Grip so much that he put him in a book (Barnaby's companion in *Barnaby Rudge*). Grip's last words, just before he died in mysterious circumstances, were "Halloa, old girl!" Mr Dickens had suspicions that the local butcher had poisoned his bird, and he was probably raven-mad at the possibility!

7 "Go home. Please."

As a small boy in Chatham, Charles was out walking with his dad, John, when they spotted a large, elegant house called Gad's Hill Place. John told Charles that if he worked very hard and became successful, he might one day own that house. Forty years later, Charles bought Gad's Hill Place. His father's prediction had come true. He got the builders in, then proudly welcomed a stream of visitors. Among them was the Danish fairy-tale writer, Hans Christian Andersen. The Dickens children (Charles had ten) must have been excited at the prospect of the famous storyteller's visit. Not for long.

Hans outstayed his welcome, hanging on far longer than the fortnight he'd been invited for, and most of the family found him rather a pain – "...a bony bore..." said Charles's daughters.

8 Wrongs to right

Mr Dickens worked hard to right wrongs. He saw much misery and injustice on his long walks, and he used his books to draw attention to the plight of the needy. As he began to hit the headlines, he wrote articles and made speeches. People listened as he demanded clean water and proper sewers, instead of stinking ditches. He campaigned against public hangings – "the great black ghastly gallows" – and claimed that capital punishment

was useless as a deterrent. He told of a clergyman who had interviewed over a hundred and fifty convicts under sentence of death. Only three had never watched an execution. All the others had seen at least one, and it hadn't put them off committing crimes. Dickens campaigned against solitary confinement in prisons, and against bad schools. Having visited the US, he loathed slavery. He also hated the American habit of spitting tobacco juice! In *Martin Chuzzlewit*, he wrote of a man who, "...smoking and chewing as he came along, and spitting frequently, recorded his progress by a train of decomposed tobacco on the ground". By making people more aware of the problems in the world around them Dickens's writing made a difference. He lived to see improvements in housing and sanitation, and the abolition of public executions. But spitters still spat.

9 The end
Dynamic Mr Dickens always put maximum effort into everything he did. The public readings he gave were tough going, partly because of the strain of acting out horrific murders and suchlike night after night, but also because of the travelling between gigs. No helicopters, no planes, no stretch limos, remember!

In 1865, Charles was involved in a terrible railway accident in Staplehurst, Kent, when many passengers

were killed. The injured had to wait a long time for medical help to arrive, for there were no high-speed emergency services in Victorian times. Charles helped and comforted the wounded as much as he could, but the whole experience had a shocking effect on him. (After helping the wounded, Dickens remembered he'd left the manuscript of his latest book, *Our Mutual Friend*, in his coat pocket. He climbed back into the train to rescue it. That handwritten manuscript would have been the only copy he had!)

He had several bouts of illness during the next few years and his health began to fail while he was still only in his fifties. However, being the man he was, he worked right up until the day before his death on 9 June 1870. He was buried at Westminster Abbey five days later. It was no surprise that people from all walks of life mourned this great man, and thousands travelled to London to pay their respects to the  "inimitable" Charles Dickens. His daughter, Mamie, told of finding flowers from unknown admirers on his grave every June, and every Christmas Day.

10 Christmas

Christmas as we know it today is very much influenced by Charles Dickens. It's almost impossible to read about the Cratchits' dinner without sharing their feelings of warmth and love (*and* without drooling). Dickensian Christmases caught on, and are the basis of our celebrations today. The very first Christmas cards were produced in 1843 – the year *A Christmas Carol* was published. You'll find that many of the Christmas cards people send today portray the sort of festivities Dickens described. He believed that the true spirit of Christmas can draw people, not just families, together and, in one of his *Sketches*, he wrote, "There seems a magic in the very name of Christmas." Dickens wanted his readers to keep the spirit of Christmas every day of their lives, not just once a year on 25 December, and that is the message in *A Christmas Carol*.

Story 9: The Pickwick Papers

In 1836 Charles Dickens was asked to write a few stories to fit some sporting illustrations, but he thought that was a duff idea. The pictures, he reckoned, should come out of the text, not the other way around.

Luckily, he got his way; and we got our number nine story – *The Pickwick Papers*. Like all his novels, it was published in monthly instalments first. This meant that the story was told in episodes, bit by bit, rather like a modern soap-opera. This was handy for Dickens as he could tell by the sales figures how much the public liked the story. For instance, when a servant called Sam Weller appeared, he was so popular that sales rocketed. Dickens would have known better than to kill Sam off! *The Pickwick Papers* was eventually published as a complete book when the author was still only 25.

The aim of Pickwick Club members was to go out and about, and to write up their observations "of character and manners, and of the whole of their adventures". Very much the sort of thing Dickens himself did in his walks around night-time London!

Some of the adventures of the Pickwickians (as Pickwick Club members were called) were quite outrageous. How might one of Sam Weller's descendants view their antics today? Have a peep at Tracy Weller's school project on "A Member of My Family"…

My Project

This is me, Tracy Samantha Augusta Natalie Weller. (I'll explain my name later.)

This project is about my great-great-great-great-uncle, Sam Weller, and the Pickwick Club.

Sam was only a servant but he was popular and very loyal and, in my opinion, the cleverest of all the Pickwickians.

Sam was a member of…

THE PICKWICK CLUB

Well, almost…

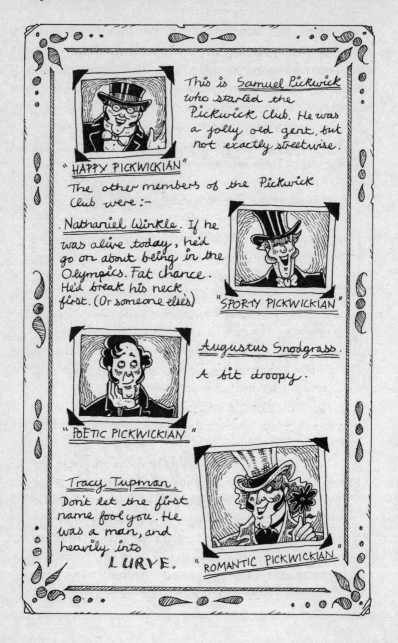

This is <u>Samuel Pickwick</u> who started the Pickwick Club. He was a jolly old gent, but not exactly streetwise.

"<u>HAPPY PICKWICKIAN</u>"

The other members of the Pickwick Club were :-

<u>Nathaniel Winkle</u>. If he was alive today, he'd go on about being in the Olympics. Fat chance. He'd break his neck first. (Or someone else's)

"<u>SPORTY PICKWICKIAN</u>"

<u>Augustus Snodgrass</u>.

A bit droopy.

"<u>POETIC PICKWICKIAN</u>"

<u>Tracy Tupman</u>. Don't let the first name fool you. He was a man, and heavily into LURVE.

"<u>ROMANTIC PICKWICKIAN</u>"

36

The first journey and a fateful meeting

The members of the Pickwick Club travelled around "discovering things" and writing about them. An excuse for a good time, in my opinion. They were described as being "as brisk as bees, if not altogether light as fairies". Sam Weller kept a record of their adventures. This is how it began.

On his way to Rochester, Samuel Pickwick questioned the coachman about everything, even the age of his horse, and made notes for the first Pickwick Paper. At the first coach stop Tupman, Winkle and Snodgrass – the rest of the Pickwickians – were waiting. When the coachman realized Mr Pickwick had written down his answers, he freaked out, accusing him of being a police spy. "I'll give it him," he cried, knocking Mr Pickwick's specs off, "even if I get six months for it." He thumped Snodgrass's eye, punched Tupman's tummy and winded Winkle.

Luckily, along came a man called Alfred Jingle who sorted everything out, and sent that coachman packing.

The Pickwickians and their new friend, Jingle, set off for the Bull Inn, Rochester. On the way, Jingle told stories – or lies – like about a woman whose head got knocked off as she rode under a bridge in a carriage. She was eating a sandwich. Another story was about all the lovers he'd had – thousands! One poisoned herself. (I'm not surprised. I'd take poison if I had to marry Jingle.)

Shots at Dingley Dell

The Pickwickians headed for Manor Farm, Dingley Dell, to stay with Tupman's friends, the Wardles.

Mr Wardle, his sister Rachael and daughters Isabella and Emily.

Tupman invited Jingle, too. (Big mistake.)

They held a shooting party. Winkle, the so-called sportsman, couldn't hit a thing. He did manage to put a bullet into Tracy Tupman's arm, though. Wardle's sister Rachael nursed Tupman, and he fell in L♥O♥V♥E with her. Unfortunately, Jingle got wind that Rachael was an heiress, and started being all lovey-dovey with her. And the next thing was...

THE DINGLEY DELL GAZETTE

Will wedding bells jangle for Jingle?

Local heiress elopes

At the White Hart, London

Mr Wardle, Mr Pickwick and poor Tupman chased after Rachael and Jingle, and finally arrived at the White Hart Inn, London, where the Boots, whose job it is to clean the guests' boots (durr!), just happened to be my ancestor, SAM WELLER!

Sam's yer man!

Mr Pickwick asked who was staying in the inn, and Sam replied, "There's a wooden leg in number 6, a pair of Wellingtons a good deal worn, and a pair of lady's shoes in number 5."

"By Heavens, we've found them," said Mr Wardle. (I don't think he meant the wooden leg.)

Alfred Jingle was trapped, and Mr Wardle told his sister, "Get on your bonnet." He had a go at them both and when he let slip that Rachael was fifty years old if she was an hour, she fainted. Mr Pickwick sent for a glass of water, but Mr Wardle cried, "A glass! Bring a bucket, and throw it all over her." (They didn't.)

Mr Jingle agreed to forget marrying Rachael if Wardle paid him £120, which was a lot in those days.

A new job for Sam

Mr Pickwick was so impressed with MY great-great-great-great-uncle, Sam, that he employed him as his manservant (best thing he ever did, as you'll see), and arranged to meet him a week later at his London lodgings.

This is Mrs Bardell, Mr Pickwick's land-lady in London.

Mrs Bardell's son, Tommy, aged 10. Horrible (in my opinion).

A misunderstanding

Mr Pickwick tried to tell Mrs Bardell that Sam was coming to live there. "Do you think it a greater expense to keep two people," he began, "than to keep one?"

"La, Mr Pickwick," she said, blushing, "what a question!" (She thought he was proposing!)

"I have made up my mind," he said.

She was crimson now, and trembling. "Oh, you're very kind, sir."

"Your little boy will have a companion," said Mr Pickwick, "who'll teach him more tricks in a week than he would learn in a year."

"Oh, you kind, good, playful dear," she cried, still thinking he was proposing, and flung herself at him. Then, just as his friends turned up, she fainted! In his arms!

(This is not the end of that episode.)

A shock for Mr Pickwick

Before his next journey, Mr Pickwick got a letter from Mrs Bardell's solicitors, Dodson and Fogg.

DODSON AND FOGG

Bardell v. Pickwick.

Sir,

Having been instructed by Mrs Bardell to commence action against you for a breach of promise of marriage, for which the plaintiff lays her damages at £1,500, we beg to inform you that a writ has been issued against you in the Court, and we request to know the name of your attorney in London.

We are, sir, your obedient servants,

Dodson and Fogg.

Mr Pickwick told the "obedient servants" that they were swindlers, and refused to pay. He was about to get physical with them, when good old Sam Weller hauled him out of harm's way.

(This is still not the end of Mrs Bardell.)

Pickwickian romances

At this point, I'll bring you up-to-date on who fancies who, because the Pickwickians are a romantic lot on the whole.

Snodgrass loves flirty Emily Wardle.

Winkle is crackers about Emily's friend, Arabella Allen. Arabella's brother's friend, Bob Sawyer, loves Arabella.

Bob hates Winkle

Samuel Pickwick is mad about Mrs Bardell (really mad, not in love).

Isabella Wardle has married Mr Trundle.

Sam Weller hadn't been wasting time either. He'd fallen for Mary, a pretty housemaid.

Disaster!

> Fleet Prison,
> London
>
> Dear Fellow Pickwickians,
>   I begin to regret my own stupidity. My refusal to pay Mrs Bardell's damages has resulted in my imprisonment in the Fleet prison, in London. My consolation is that my loyal, trusted servant, Sam, has so arranged

Matters (I cannot imagine how) that he has had himself committed to prison, so he may continue serving me. What a man!

Believe it or not, that rascal Jingle is here too. At last he has got what he deserves. However, I cannot see him starve, so will help him – to emigrate.

But, I ask you, my friends, do I deserve this?

Your friend,
Samuel Pickwick

Didn't I tell you Sam Weller was the best?

Fleet Prison,
London

Dear Fellow Pickwickians,
Great news! Mrs Bardell's in prison! (Sorry, those are not the words of a true gentleman, but you will excuse me when you know the latest events.) Mrs Bardell didn't pay her own court costs and now she's in the Fleet as well! I have offered to pay

them for her, if she agrees to forget the damages I owe (hah!) her.

We leave the Fleet today, my loyal Sam and I. your friend,

Samuel Pickwick

Romance update

Nathaniel Winkle married Arabella in secret.

His dad was furious. Arabella's brother was hopping mad, but Mr Pickwick smoothed their feathers.

Augustus Snodgrass married Emily Wardle.

They settled at Dingley Dell.

Tracy Tupman, the great lover, was so upset at Rachael eloping with Jingle after she'd seemed keen on him, that he never, ever married.

Jingle ended up unloved. He emigrated.

Mr Pickwick retired to Dulwich.

And my great-great-great-great-uncle, Sam Weller? Loyal to the end, he lived with Mr Pickwick and looked after him. But he wasn't alone. Oh, no. Remember Mary, the housemaid? Soon there were wedding bells and it wasn't long before there was the patter of tiny feet.

And although Mr Pickwick became older and not so fit, the little boys adored him, because he was always young at heart.

My name? All Sam Weller's descendants have been named after the members of the Pickwick Club – me too, and I'm proud of it.

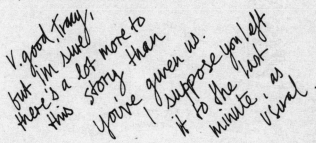

V. good, Tracy, but I'm sure there's a lot more to this story than you've given us. I suppose you left it to the last minute, as usual.

Rotten egg: Alfred Jingle

"Mr Jingle knew that young men, to spinster aunts, are as lighted gas to gunpowder, and he determined to essay the effect of an explosion without loss of time."

Good egg: Samuel Pickwick

"He would not deny that he was influenced by human passions, and human feelings ... possibly by human weaknesses ... but this he would say, that if ever the fire of self-importance broke out in his bosom, the desire to benefit the human race in preference effectually quenched it."

Top Facts 9: Victorian servants

Sam Weller was a gentleman's servant, and enjoyed the benefits of travelling round the country with his master. He was treated with affection and respect by Mr Pickwick. Often servants were not treated so well.

In many great houses, the master and mistress might not even recognize their lowliest scullery maid if they bumped into her in the street. (Not likely. She'd leap into the gutter to let a fine lady pass.) That maid would rarely be seen in the mistress's rooms, unless she was cleaning out the fireplace, in which case, the mistress would be elsewhere.

Let's imagine you're looking for a job as a kitchen maid. This looks a likely one:

KITCHEN MAID WANTED

Live in, good food, flexible hours, ample free time, uniform provided, well-furnished house, varied duties, nursery staff kept. No followers.

Apply, with references, to Lady Lowerleigh

Looks good, eh? Hmmm. Let's take a closer look:

1 Live in

"In" is true. They don't mention "up" and "down". Take this job and you'll spend nearly all day in the basement, and climb the back stairs late at night to sleep in the attic. Your bedroom will have a bed, chair, wash basin and maybe a small chest of drawers. The cook, butler, governess and lady's maid live much more comfortably and have other servants to help them.

2 Good food

True, and you'll have a lot to do with it! There's no fridge or freezer, so food is bought fresh. Tradesmen, such as the butcher, grocer and baker deliver daily. If Lady Luvverleigh's household is large enough, it will have its own kitchen garden, supplying fresh vegetables. You'll have to scrub, peel and chop them. Everything is cooked from scratch – nothing's "instant". Cook produces several lavish meals a day for upstairs, and three meals a day for the below-stairs staff. As you'll do all the dirty work, you'll be busy helping her!

"Now the tongue – now the pigeon-pie. Take care of that veal and ham – mind the lobsters – take the salad out of the cloth – give me the dressing."

Pickwick Papers

3 Flexible hours

Flexible for them, not for you. All servants have long working days, but you, being young and unskilled, will have the worst hours of the lot. You might have to be up as early as 5 *a.m.* to get the cooking range going and heat water. You might have the odd early night and finish by 10 p.m., but it will often be much later. Think yourself lucky – a coachman might only have the horses and carriage to look after, but he's on call twenty-four hours a day!

4 Ample free time
Oh, yeah? Don't start worrying about what to do on your day off. You'll be fortunate if you have one! There aren't any fixed days off. Weekends will mean nothing to you except maybe a brief rest in church on Sunday. If Lady Luvverleigh's a good employer, you may get an occasional afternoon off but, don't forget, some people only get *one* day off a year – Christmas Day.

5 Uniform provided
Suspicious, this. It won't matter what you wear in the kitchen – anything drab and practical will do, because nobody who matters ever sees you. However, if Lady L wants you to double up as parlour maid, you'll need a black dress, a snowy apron and crisp white cap, i.e. uniform. You can't rush from fetching coal to pouring tea for the mistress's guests without changing. All servants dress to suit their positions. For instance, a footman opens the front door and waits at table, so he wears a fancy uniform called livery. Just be glad you don't work for a poorer family who can only afford to employ a "general": a maid who does everything – upstairs, downstairs and in the lady's chamber. If you

had different outfits for the kitchen, for housework and for waiting at table, you could easily make a mistake!

6 Well-furnished house

Bound to be. Victorians are champion hoarders. Lady L's drawing-room will be plastered with knick-knacks: vases, ornaments, china bowls, glass dishes, framed photos, potted plants (large), little boxes, albums of pressed flowers, embroidery frames, books, pens, ink pots, doilies, clocks... Of course, all these objects need something to stand on, so there'll be shelves, an overmantel above the fireplace, a piano and several cloth-covered tables. Some Victorians have so much gear that they run out of surfaces! Never fear – there's a special piece of furniture that's made just to hold clutter. By this time they've also run out of names for furniture, so they call it a whatnot. All this stuff has to be dusted. Who by? It could be you...

7 Varied duties

When you have your interview try to find out what this means. She probably won't say. Just accept that you'll be expected to be versatile. The jobs you might have to tackle include washing up, scrubbing, polishing, dusting, washing, ironing, cooking, serving, making beds, fetching coal, emptying rubbish, making tea... You could do yourself a favour by becoming nifty with a sewing needle. In the dead of winter it's cosier to sit by the fire mending petticoats than scraping ice from the front doorstep!

"Only two in our kitchen ... cook and 'ousemaid. We keep a boy to do the dirty work, and a gal besides, but they dine in the washus."

The Pickwick Papers

8 Nursery staff kept
That sounds OK. If Lady Luvverleigh's wealthy, her kids will have a nanny, nursery nurse, and governess. The Luvverleigh nursery staff will have other servants to call on. There might be both a day and night nursery, next to the nanny's sitting-room. The children see their parents only occasionally. The nursery staff deal with everything: clothes, manners, lessons, manners, playtimes and walks. And more manners. Nanny and the nurse eat "nursery food" with the children: lots of boiled things and milky puddings.

9 No followers
OK. You're a maid. You'd like to get married, maybe have a few kids. Unless there's a young footman at Lady Luvverleigh's who gives you the eye, forget it. It'll be harder to find a boyfriend than fly to the moon (and you

know perfectly well *that's* impossible). How do you meet a man when the only place you go is home to Mum on your afternoon off? Even if you do meet one, when will you see him? You can't slip out for half an hour, and Cook won't allow what she calls "followers". And if Cook says, "No", that's law! If you want to improve your life, it's best to work hard, become assistant cook, or maybe even *the* cook. Then at least you might catch yourself a butler.

10 Apply, with references
If you take this job, you'd better keep your nose clean. You've no choice but to obey Lady L. There are no contracts of employment or trades unions to protect your rights. Basically, you have no rights. If you're reckless enough to break a rule, you could be fired instantly. That would mean no job, no home, and no wages. There's no unemployment benefit to tide you over until you get another job – *if* you get another job. Being fired means leaving without a written reference saying what a good, honest worker you are. Without that reference you're unlikely to get another job.

"Here the cook began to cry, and the housemaid said it was 'a shame!' for which partisanship she received a month's warning on the spot."

The Pickwick Papers

How different were the lives of mistress and maid. Let's look at an imaginary ten hours in the life of Lady Luvverleigh and her servant, Elsie Scrubb…

Lady Luvverleigh

Breakfast of ham, eggs, toast, bacon, kidneys, porridge (not all on the same plate).

Read the paper, yawn a lot, do embroidery.

Change clothes, go riding or visit friends.

Elsie Scrubb

9 a.m.

Up since 6 a.m. working through a job list: wash, wake other servants, heat water, blacklead the cooking range, light fire. Lay fires in other rooms, put porridge on, take hot water to bedrooms, stir porridge, polish front door knocker. Help Cook with breakfast, empty chamber pots, eat breakfast.

10 a.m.

Scrape out porridge pot, wash up, clean the kitchen, help make the beds.

11 a.m.

Peel spuds, chop carrots, weep over onions, fetch coal, light dining-room fire.

noon

Write letters, pick flowers, change clothes.

Do the dusting, scrub floors, help cook lunch.

Have long lunch, grumble about the servants.

1p.m.
Eat lunch, wash up, scrub kitchen table.

Visit dressmaker.

2p.m.
Clean windows, help Cook make cakes.

Buy hat to match new dress.

3p.m.
Fetch coal, darn stockings, mend Cook's petticoat.

Change clothes, have tea and gossip with friends.

4p.m.
Have tea, wash tea things, enjoy free time.

5 p.m.

Rest, read thrilling novel.

Help Cook with dinner.

6 p.m.

Bath and dress for dinner; silks, satins, jewels, the lot.

Wash up Cook's pots and pans, lay table for servants' dinner. Do ironing.

7 p.m.

Have dinner. Visit theatre, or stay home and play the piano, sing songs, read, play games before bed.

Light fires in bedrooms, eat dinner, wash up servants' dinner things, wash up dinner things from upstairs, scrub kitchen table, fetch coal, go to bed at 11 p.m.

Story 8: Dombey & Son

Charles Dickens wrote *Dombey & Son*, coming in at Top Ten story number eight, against the background of the new railways, which were changing the face of the land.

It's the story of a family with more problems than friends. Mr Dombey himself is a cold, proud man who cares only for money, success and his son and heir, little Paul.

His devoted daughter, Florence, relies on her sharp-tongued maid, Susan Nipper, for companionship. Who else could she confide in?

Let's listen in as Susan entertains an old friend to tea…

Tea for Toots

Susan: Come in – door's open. We haven't had a good chat in years. Get the weight off your feet and we'll have a cuppa. Pop the kettle on first, will you? The cat's asleep on my lap.

Mary: You promised to dish the dirt about those Dombeys.

Susan: Give you the goss, I said, not dish the dirt. And don't rush me. Where did it all start?

Mary: You were Florence Dombey's maid, weren't you?

Susan: We called her Miss Floy. It was her little brother's name for her.

Mary: She had a brother?

Susan: She did. Master Paul was the "Son" in Dombey & Son. Dear little chap. Sweet as plum jam, and the apple of Mr Dombey's eye. The most important thing in the world to him, Master Paul was.

Mary: And Florence of course.

Susan: You're kidding! Mr Dombey might not have had a daughter, for all the love he ever showed Miss Floy. He only cared about Paul, heir to the great London firm of Dombey & Son. Mrs Dombey died after Paul was born, when Miss Floy was about six. The last sounds Mrs Dombey heard were her little girl's sobs and the words, "Oh dear Mamma!"

Mary: Poor love.

Susan: Mr Dombey needed a nurse for the baby, so Polly Toodle moved in. She had strict instructions never to visit her own family while she was Master Paul's nurse. Her sister looked after Mr Toodle and the children.

Mary: Didn't she miss them?

Susan: Something chronic.

Mary: Did you get on OK with Polly?

Susan: We had a bit of a ding-dong the first time we met. Miss Floy and I went away after Mrs Dombey died. When we got back, Polly let Miss Floy see Master Paul

– that was right against Mr Dombey's orders. And I remember Polly saying, "Miss Florence will be so pleased to see her dear papa tonight." Fat lot she knew! "Her pa's a deal too wrapped up in somebody else," I said. "Girls are thrown away in this house."

Mary: You didn't.

Susan: I did. We got on fine once she realized you don't mess with Susan Nipper. She was a good nurse. Even the Master thought so. In fact, he rewarded her by sending Biler to school.

Mary: Biler?

Susan: Her son. His real name was Robin, but they called him after some steam engine. Polly's husband worked on the new railway.

Everyone was railway-mad at the time. Mad's the word, if you ask me. Dirty, smelly, dangerous things.

Mary: Dangerous?

Susan: I'll come to that later. Perhaps I should have steered clear of poor Polly. Trouble was just round the corner, 'cos of us getting on well. She was desperate to see Biler before he went off to school, so I suggested she paid a visit home.

Mary: Against the rules.

Susan: Against the rules. But, like I told Polly, what the eye don't see… I also said, out of the goodness of my heart, me and Miss Floy would walk with her. Oh lor, that decision caused Miss Floy a lot of grief – and, strangely, a lot of happiness. Kettle's boiling.

Mary: Shall I make the tea?

Susan: Blimey, no. You're a guest, aren't you? But if you could pass me that blue teapot … I can't quite reach it.

Mary: Here. What was Polly's house like?

Susan: Small. Crowded. What you'd expect. Pop some water in the pot to warm it, there's a love. You're nearest. All round her street they were digging up and knocking down and bashing about to make a new railway line. Hard to keep the dust down. Anyway, Polly's boy, Biler, wasn't back from school. When he did come, some kids chased him, taking the mick out of his uniform and stuff. Then some idiot shouted, "Mad bull!" and people went crazy. Like a riot. Hundreds of them.

Mary: Hundreds?

Susan: Seemed like hundreds. Drain the pot, Mary, there's a dear, and pass the tea tin. Anyway, in the middle of all the fighting and people running about, Miss Floy vanished.

Mary: You must have gone mad!
Susan: I did!
Mary: Shall I put some tea in the pot before it goes cold?

Susan: Please. Well, you can imagine the hoo-ha back at Dombey's when they found out I'd lost one of the family.

Mary: What happened to her?

Susan: I discovered afterwards that a horrible old woman, calling herself Good Mrs Brown – about as good as a rotten apple stewed with slugs and earwigs, if you ask me – offered to take Miss Floy back to me, but instead she took her home, stole her clothes and sent her back on the street in rags!

Mary: She didn't.

Susan: She did. Miss Floy, being a bright kid, tried to find her dad's office. The incredible thing is that the first person she asked had been talking, *not two minutes before*, to a lad called Walter Gay, who worked for Mr Dombey!

Mary: No!

Susan: Yes! He lived at the Wooden Midshipman, where his uncle, Solomon Gills, sold ships' instruments. Walter took Miss Floy home, and Uncle Sol cared for her while Walter let us know she was safe. I was never so relieved in my life. Walter took me to fetch her, and when I got back Mr Dombey fired poor Polly.

Mary: What about you?

Susan: Mr Dombey blamed Polly for leading me astray, when it was all my ... all my fault for ... for taking Miss Floy ... and ... and...

Mary: Don't get upset. Here, let me pour you a cuppa.

Susan: Thanks, dear.

Mary: Change the subject. What about Master Paul?

Susan: He missed Polly Toodle something chronic, but he and Miss Floy loved each other to bits. He was a weak little thing and, when he was about five, one of his doctors recommended sea air for his health. He went to stay at Mrs Pipchin's in Brighton. It wasn't exactly a school – it was known as an "infantine boarding-house of a very select description".

Mary: Very posh.

Susan: Put the biscuit tin on the table, Mary. Miss Floy and me went to stay in Brighton, too. About a year later, Mr Dombey came down and arranged for Master Paul to go to Dr Blimber's school.

Mary: Was it dreadful?

Susan: Not dreadful, but if you want my opinion, and nobody did just then, it was all too *hard* for the poor lad. Miss Floy visited him every weekend. Bless her, she sent me out to buy the same schoolbooks as Master Paul had, so she could help him with his work.

Mary: Are we having a biscuit, Susan, dear?

Susan: Sorry! Pass me the tin. There was one good thing about the school. Toots!

Mary: Toots?

61

Susan: Toots! Can *you* get this lid off? I can't.

Mary: Give it here. What's Toots?

Susan: Toots was sort of head boy. He was kind to Master Paul, and he soon took a fancy to little Miss Floy, he did.

Mary: Ooh, I like a romance, I do.

Susan: I can tell you now, miss, there was no romance between Toots and Miss Floy! She was only about fourteen. No one gave a thought to any such thing at that time, because Master Paul became weaker, and just faded away.

Mary: Oh no! You mean…?

Susan: He died. It was awful. When it happened, it seemed to me that the whole world was crying. I can't … I can't talk … about it … without … c-crying…

Mary: There now. Have a custard cream.

Susan: Thanks, dear. Well, Miss Floy and Walter Gay – I wasn't supposed to know this, but I've got big ears – swore to love each other as brother and sister, for ever. Poor darling, apart from me, she had no one else. You'd have thought her father would have found her a comfort in his grief, but no – he turned away from her, as if she didn't exist.

Mary: Poor Florence. She couldn't have had a sadder life.

Susan: It got sadder. Mr Dombey's manager, Carker, arranged for Walter to be sent to work in the West Indies. He sailed on the *Son and Heir* and Miss Floy was alone. Oh, I forgot the dog.

Mary: Dog?

Susan: Diogenes. Master Paul used to play with him at school, and Toots, bless him, brought it to Miss Floy as a sort of keepsake, he said. Sweet.

Mary: Did Mr Dombey pine away?

Susan: Not him! He married again, a woman called Edith Granger. That marriage was a big mistake. She was too proud and strong to let herself be ordered about by Mr Dombey. They never got on. I liked her though, because she tried to be a mother to Miss Floy. In fact, Miss Floy called her "Mamma" from the start. Edith tried to make Mr Dombey see what a treasure Florence was, but it was like talking to a brick wall. It made her mad.

Mary: His loss.

Susan: Course. They were always falling out, those two – at it like fighting cocks most nights, till Edith took to her room and cut herself off from everybody. Mr Dombey sent messages to her through Carker, rather than speak to her. That was a mistake!

Mary: Why?

Susan: Tell you in a sec. I'd seen a newspaper report that the *Son and Heir* was lost at sea. I got Toots to go to Solomon Gills's to see if it was true.

Mary: Was it?

Susan: Yes. Poor Miss Floy was heartbroken. Pour me another cup, Mary, or I can't go on. The final straw was when Mr Dombey forbade Edith to have anything more to do with Miss Floy. I couldn't stand it any more. I went to him and told him how wonderful his Florence was and how devoted to him. I told him, I did, that he treated her badly and cared more for his importance and his fortune than for her.

Mary: You didn't!

Susan: I did.

Mary: What happened?

Susan: I was fired. Pick me out a digestive, will you? Toots took me to the coach and I went to stay with my brother. Before I left, Toots asked if I thought he and Miss Floy might ever make a go of it.

Mary: What? Get married? What did you say?

Susan: I told him no way, José. Forget it. Now what happened next was Edith Dombey ran away to France with Carker!

Mary: No!

Susan: Oh, she never loved Carker – it was just to escape and be revenged on Mr Dombey. After she disappeared, Miss Floy tried to comfort her dad, but he was so mad with rage he hit her.

Mary: He didn't!

Susan: He did, the swine. He called Edith a few choice names and that was it. Miss Floy ran away!

Mary: Where to?

Susan: To the one kind person she knew – Walter's Uncle Sol. But he was gone – disappeared – mad with grief for Walter. His best friend, Captain Cuttle, was taking care of things, and he was just as good to Miss Floy as old Sol would have been. And there came a night when he had to break some news to her.

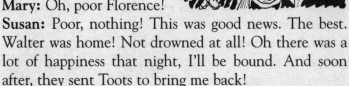

Mary: Oh, poor Florence!

Susan: Poor, nothing! This was good news. The best. Walter was home! Not drowned at all! Oh there was a lot of happiness that night, I'll be bound. And soon after, they sent Toots to bring me back!

Mary: Aah! Can I have another cup of tea?

Susan: Help yourself. Edith Dombey, once safe in France, told Carker exactly why she'd run off with him. They had a row, but Dombey turned up in the middle of it, and she ran away. Carker escaped Dombey's clutches and fled back to England, but Dombey was after him. It ended at a quiet railway station. Carker realized Dombey had caught him, panicked, and lost his footing. He fell on to the track. The last thing he saw was the red eyes of the four o'clock express, a split second before he was ripped to pieces and splattered all over the place.

Mary: Yeeuck.

Susan: I reached the Wooden Midshipman to find Miss Floy and Walter engaged. The night before the wedding, Solomon Gills turned up – he'd been off searching for Walter – and everyone was happy, except me. It near broke my heart to hear that the honeymooners were going on a long, long trip abroad – without me.

Mary: Shame. What happened to Mr Dombey?

Susan: His business went bust. Serve the old swine right, I say. He got more and more miserable – became quite a hermit – and it's my opinion he realized at last what he'd lost. Not just his money, I mean, but his daughter's love.

Mary: Is that the end of the story?

Susan: Oh, no. Miss Floy and Walter came back, with their baby son – Paul! Miss Floy went to her dad, offered her love – *again* – and asked him to forgive her. Should have been the other way round if you ask me. He was near dead, but she stayed with him. He even asked for me once, and begged me not to leave them. He said he understood why I'd said what I did, and forgave me.

Mary: Cheek.

Susan: Oh, that was Dombey – couldn't ever be in the wrong. Anyway, I think he'll get better, and I hope he and Miss Floy find happiness in each other. So that's it – you're up to date on everybody.

Mary: What about you, Susan? Did you never marry?
Susan: Me? You bet I did. That's my husband coming up the path now. Hello, Toots! Tea?

Dickens data…
The death of little Paul Dombey touched the hearts of Dickens's readers. During the nineteenth century, many women died in childbirth, and the early loss of a child was all too common. Most people had some experience of untimely death, so were deeply affected. A judge called Lord Jeffrey wrote, "Oh my dear Dickens … I have so cried and sobbed over it…"

Rotten egg: James Carker

"…of a florid complexion, and with two unbroken rows of glistening teeth, whose regularity and whiteness were quite distressing … he showed them whenever he spoke; and bore so wide a smile upon his countenance (a smile, however, very rarely, indeed, extending beyond his mouth), that there was something in it like the snarl of a cat."

Good egg: Solomon Gills

"I began to think it would be my fate to cruise about in search of tidings of my boy until I died."

Top Facts 8: Getting around

Dombey & Son is set in London when great areas were being ripped up to make way for new rail lines. Dickens described how "the first shock of a great earthquake had ... rent the whole neighbourhood to its centre... Houses were knocked down; streets broken through ... deep pits and trenches dug in the ground ... in short, the yet unfinished and unopened Railroad was in progress ... upon its mighty course of civilization and improvement."

Transport was changing people's lives. Let's look at some of the facts.

1 Where to, mate?

As long as he didn't expect to fly, the Victorian was spoilt for choice as far as transport goes. He could travel by train, stagecoach, hansom cab (known as a "growler"), or he might have his own bike or horse-drawn carriage. The Thames was a superb highway, so a boat was another option. The river was busy, but never as jam-packed as the streets of London.

2 Up, up and away...

If he could bear the traffic and the noise, the Victorian could always hop on a bus. A bus? Yes, an omnibus (the word comes from Latin, and means "for all", probably because all the people could use it, if they had the fare). Double-decker omnibuses were horse-drawn, with back-to-back seats on top (called knifeboards), and passengers climbed an iron ladder to reach them.

Omnibuses were cheaper than hansom cabs, but the poor people still couldn't afford them.

"…Snow Hill where omnibus horses going eastward seriously think of falling down on purpose…"

Nicholas Nickleby

3 Way to go

In 1825, people could travel by train for the first time. Luxury! Oh, yes? The carriages looked a lot like builders' rubbish skips and the passengers had to put up with the steam-engine's smoke, soot and whatever the weather threw at them!

4 Time after time

When clocks were set by the sun, a Londoner's midday was slightly earlier than a Welshman's so people had "local time" which varied from town to town. When railways came along, timetables couldn't be stuck to if everyone had different time, so "railway time" was invented, based on the time at Greenwich. By about 1880 clocks all over the country showed the same time – railway time.

5 Class difference

Queen Victoria's first train trip was from Paddington to Windsor in 1842. She had a sumptuous private carriage, but in the early days it was different for ordinary people.

Travel 1st class
You get a seat to sit on and a roof to shelter you.

Travel 2nd class
You get a seat, but you'd better take an umbrella.

Travel 3rd class
No seat and forget the umbrella – you need both hands to stop yourself falling out.

As time went by, everybody got a seat, even if it was only a hard wooden bench in third class.

6 Sheep jam

In the middle of the nineteenth century (like today!), London suffered horrendous traffic jams. In *Nicholas Nickleby*, Dickens wrote of "…the streets being crowded … with vehicles of every kind…" In the middle of one choking jam were an omnibus, a lady's carriage, a hansom cab, a horse and cart and a flock of sheep!

7 Have wheels, will tunnel

The streets couldn't take much more, so the world's first underground, the Metropolitan Line, was built, and opened in 1863. Travelling underground had one big advantage – you stayed dry. But you had to sit in a carriage like a wooden crate on wheels, and there was nowhere else for the steam engine's smoke, soot and smells to go except in your face!

8 I do like to be beside the seaside

The new railways were so fast that day trips to the coast were possible for most people. Small coastal towns, such as Bournemouth and Blackpool, soon developed into holiday resorts. Promenade walkways were built along the seafront and piers stretched out into the water.

9 Pedal power

The first bicycles were made of wood, with no pedals, and the rider used his feet to "walk" the bike along the ground. Later ones were more practical, but comfort wasn't top priority. Round about the middle of the century, cycling over cobbles on iron wheels caused the bike to be known as a "boneshaker". The "penny-farthing" (named after two coins), with a small rear wheel and a huge front one, appeared in the 1870s, followed by the chain-driven "safety" bicycle in the 1880s. All these bikes were hard going, because gears didn't appear until after the Victorian era.

10 Pre-fax facts

In these days of faxes, e-mails and the information superhighway, it's hard to believe that it once took days for mail to travel any distance and, even then, there was no guarantee that it would make it at all. In *The Pickwick Papers*, Dickens writes: "...though several letters were despatched, none of them ever reached my hands." We have the Victorians to thank for beginning to change all that. Here are ten pre-fax facts.

• **Free-mail** Before 1840, you could send a letter and it cost you nothing. The person you sent it to had to pay. If he or she refused, the letter was taken away.

- **Don't send loo rolls!** The amount paid was based on the distance and how many sheets of paper were used. Two sheets – double the price. (Some people would fill a page with writing, then turn it sideways and cover it again with lines going across the first lot at right angles. These letters are surprisingly easy to read.)

- **Hill-conceived idea** As people could never be sure their letters had been paid for and received, a bright schoolteacher (it can happen) named Rowland Hill suggested the sender should pay.
- **Gee-up** The new railways changed the postal services and did away with the need for horse-drawn mail coaches. Trains were much faster, and letters could be sorted on the move.
- **Royal stamp of approval** In 1840 the postage stamp was introduced. The first one was the Penny Black which had a portrait of (no, not Penny) Queen Victoria.
- **Postal dis-order** At first, letters had to be delivered and collected at the Post Office. They were bustling, busy places, often chaotic, with long queues. Some people say they haven't changed.

- **Right up your street!** Pillar boxes were introduced in London in 1855. At last, posting a letter meant just a short walk.
- **Going down the tube** An underground service was devised in 1863 for transporting mailbags between Euston train station and the North Western District Post Office. The containers were sucked along the track by a vacuum process.

- **Pass the parcel** The Post Office didn't introduce a parcel post service until 1883. It must have been most welcome.

- **Bad luck, Bonzo!** Instead of walking, postmen in the city outskirts delivered mail on penny-farthing bicycles. This made it harder for the dogs but easier for the postmen, as there were several deliveries each day.

Story 7: Hard Times

In the number seven slot is *Hard Times*, the shortest of Dickens's novels. It's set, not in London, but in sooty, industrial Coketown – a place of "machinery and tall chimneys, out of which interminable serpents of smoke trailed themselves for ever and ever, and never got uncoiled". Although Dickens invented Coketown, he based it on cities he knew.

Life was good for the wealthy factory and mill owners. The workers were the ones who *really* had the hard times. Dickens wanted to bring the conditions suffered by the workers to the attention of his readers. He vowed "to strike the heaviest blow in my power" for the workers, and trust him to wrap it all up in a jolly good story.

The Gradgrind family, so superior to circus girl, Sissy Jupe, could never have imagined how much she would mean to them. Sissy herself, a gentle, loving girl, was just like the rest of us. She knew what was right and what was wrong. If they'd had true confession magazines in Sissy's day, perhaps that's how she'd have spilled the beans about the Bad Thing she did…

I Helped A Bank Robber To Escape!

SISSY JUPE'S TRUE CONFESSION

How it all began

I'm not a bad girl. I've always tried to be good, but I once did a Bad Thing.

It started with Mr Gradgrind, the school governor. He thought I was stupid. He only believed in Facts, you see. Facts, Facts and more Facts. He wanted to turn us all into Facts machines.

Mr Gradgrind: Grinds on and on about Facts, Facts, Facts.

"Girl number 20," he said, even though my name is Sissy Jupe, "give me your definition of a horse." Now, as my dad was a riding clown in Sleary's Horseriding Circus, I do know about horses.

My dad: Being a clown meant he fell off a lot!

But before I could answer, he asked pasty-faced Bitzer instead.

Bitzer: Bit of a bully and bit of a creep.

Course, Bitzer came out with a string of – you guessed it – Facts.

That's not how I see a horse!

At that moment, I hated Bitzer, I hated my school, and I hated the town. Here are some Facts for you. COKETOWN: smelly, filthy, stinky, smoky, grimy factories, noisy mills.

Even back at the circus (Facts: happy, noisy with laughter and music, friendly, exciting) I couldn't escape the grim Gradgrind family. I spotted young Louisa and Tom Gradgrind, peeping through a hole in a fence.

Louisa: Posh, but nice. Tom: Crafty, and not so nice.

Suddenly, Mr Gradgrind pounced.

"Louisa! Tom!" he bellowed. "What do you do here?"

"Wanted to see what it was like," said Louisa. She told him she'd made her brother come, too.

But guess who got the blame? Me! Apparently, my

being in the school was having a bad effect on Louisa and Tom.

The day didn't get any better. I went off to buy some ointment for Dad's bruises from where he falls off his horse, and mouldy Bitzer started chasing me. Desperate to shake him off, I almost ran into Mr Gradgrind and his friend Josiah Bounderby.

Bounderby: Mill and bank owner – "Bound-to-be" trouble!
They'd come to see Dad. Terrified, I took them to our room over the Pegasus Arms. I knew they'd come about me but what had I done? It must have been something bad, but

I couldn't think what. I reckoned Gradgrind was going to have me expelled.

He dumped me!
It was far, far worse! So horrible to remember, it still makes me cry, even after all these years. Dad wasn't there. According to Mr Sleary, who turned up with some of the circus people, he had gone. Vanished! His dog, Merrylegs, was gone, too, so I knew it was true.

I'd been abandoned. Deserted. Dumped. They told me Dad's work had gone off, that he was ashamed for me to see him fail. I just hoped that was true. I couldn't bear it if he'd left me because he didn't want me.

After a lot of yakking from Mr Bounderby, about what a hard upbringing he'd had, and how he'd been deserted by his mother, Mr Gradgrind offered to take me into his home, and let me continue with school.

Mr Sleary said I could stay with the circus people, but Mr Gradgrind banged on about the importance of education.

Mrs Sparsit: Reckons Bounderby's not so dusty!

Mr Sleary: Kind circus owner who likes his tipple.

What should I do? I was forced to make up my mind – and quickly. Finally, I took Mr Gradgrind's offer. I had to think of my future. There wasn't anyone else to think of it for me, was there?

My strange new home

I was taken first to Mr Bounderby's. His housekeeper, Mrs Sparsit, was all smarmy when he was around. I wasn't fooled. She fancied him – or rather, his money.

Later, Mr Gradgrind brought Miss Louisa to collect me. All the way home, she never spoke. Stuck-up cat, I thought.

I wasn't unhappy at Stone Lodge. Mrs Gradgrind was like a little, thin, white, pink-eyed bundle of shawls, forever swigging medicine.

Mrs Gradgrind: Weak body and brain to match.

Miss Louisa turned out to be OK. I was never sure about Master Tom.

School was hard going.

School Report
Name: Sissy Jupe.
Facts: Knows none.
History: Past caring.
Geography: Gets lost.
Mathematics: Less than good.
English: Can speak it.
General: Wonders too much. Should face facts.
Signed: Mr M'Choakumchild Schoolmaster.

All the time I hoped and hoped my dad would come back.

I hated Bounderby!

Years passed. Master Tom went off to work at Mr Bounderby's bank. I finished my schooling and carried on helping Mrs Gradgrind. It wasn't a bad life.

Then one day Mr Gradgrind told Miss Louisa, who'd grown into a fine young lady, that Mr Bounderby wanted to marry her. And she said, "Yes"! Well, you could have knocked me down with a fly-swat! How could she? Great puffed-up windbag, he was, always bragging about what a hard time he'd had. I hated Bounderby.

Louisa and Bounderby marry!

The one person who was really pleased about this union was Master Tom. I could see his thinking, and his thoughts weren't for Miss Louisa. Oh no, he reckoned he'd be far better off at the bank when he became brother-in-law to the owner.

I was right about Mrs Sparsit, though. She was upset about the marriage. She wanted to be Mrs Bounderby. She was allowed to keep her job, but she had to move to rooms over the bank.

Hunk on the scene

About a year after the wedding, James Harthouse came to Coketown.

James Harthouse: Hunk.

Instantly, Harthouse fell for Miss Louisa, or Mrs Bounderby, as she now was. This was not good news. He was smart enough to see that Louisa really cared about Tom, so he made friends with him. Tom, by now, was a cunning young man – he gambled, drank and sponged off Louisa.

I suspect a trick

About this time, Stephen Blackpool appeared on the scene.

Stephen Blackpool: Soon to be prime suspect.

He loved a woman called Rachael, but was already married to a vile, drunken, horrible, revolting woman. Stephen worked in Bounderby's mill, and was having some bother with his workmates. Bounderby fired him. Getting the sack in Coketown was bad news. If one mill owner wouldn't employ you, no one would. Louisa and Tom went to see him. Louisa gave Stephen some money, which was kind, and Tom told him, in private, to hang around the bank. He, Tom, might be able to help him.

If you think Tom had something sneaky in mind, you're dead right. Poor Stephen waited in hope outside the bank. For nothing. Tragic, really – he'd had his hopes built up, only to have them knocked down.

Not long after, James Harthouse (who'd been hanging around Louisa a lot) went home to find Mr Bounderby going berserk because his bank had been robbed.

Robbed: Bounderby berserk!

Mrs Sparsit moved back into the Bounderby house to "get over the shock" (get back in with Mr Bounderby, if you ask me). It seemed she and Bitzer, who was now the bank's porter, suspected Stephen Blackpool. Time for Stephen to disappear.

Where was the pain?
One sad day, we sent a note to Louisa Bounderby.

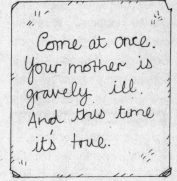

Come at once. Your mother is gravely ill. And this time it's true.

Louisa raced to Stone Lodge. "Are you in pain, dear mother?" she cried.

"I think there's a pain somewhere in the room," said Mrs Gradgrind, "but I couldn't positively say that I have got it."

Well, she had got it, and she died soon after, but not before hinting that she realized something valuable was missing from her children's lives. Poor soul. Anyone could see what was missing. Feelings, emotion, passion, that's what was missing. What Mr Gradgrind called "Fancy".

Goings-on

I know that Louisa spent time with Mr Harthouse. What they were up to, I can't imagine. Well, I can. Goings-on, I call it, but one person knew for sure. Spying Sparsit – troublemaker!

Sneaky Sparsit spied on Louisa and Harthouse.

She still spent weekends at the house, and one day she heard just what she wanted to hear – Louisa and Mr Harthouse planning to elope that night! Sparsit couldn't wait to spill the beans.

But Louisa didn't elope. She came home to Stone Lodge, instead, and confessed everything to her father – how unhappy she was in her marriage, how she'd nearly eloped – the lot. She's so sensible – and so good. Not like me...

She stayed in her old room, and I looked after her, poor darling. I saw to everything. I even plucked up courage and went to sort out Mr Harthouse. "You'll never see Miss Louisa again!" I told him. He got my message all right – did the decent thing and left Coketown.

Prime suspect

Mrs Sparsit, meanwhile, knew nothing about Louisa's

confession. She followed Bounderby to London and told him – smugly, I bet – that Louisa had eloped. They charged back to Stone Lodge to see Gradgrind. Hah! They soon discovered the truth. No elopement. That wiped the grin off Sparsit's face. Mr Bounderby ordered Louisa to return home by noon next day. Or else.

She didn't, of course, so that was that. Marriage over. Good job, too.

Bounderby, meanwhile, offered a reward for Stephen Blackpool's arrest.

Standing outside the bank (at Tom's suggestion, remember)

had made him the prime suspect.

Horror at Old Hell

Stephen's friend, Rachael, and I were walking in the countryside near Coketown when we stumbled across a broken fence, and found a hat near by. Stephen's hat! Rachael went berserk. We were on the edge of Old Hell mine shaft. Poor Stephen must be lying at the bottom.

We sent for help. Everyone came to Old Hell mine – Mr Bounderby, Mr Gradgrind, Tom – even Louisa. Eventually, poor Stephen was brought to the surface. It was ghastly. He was dreadfully injured.

Dying words: Stephen gasped to Mr Gradgrind.

Before he died, he asked Mr Gradgrind to clear his name of suspicion. "Your son will tell you how," Stephen groaned.

Suddenly, it all became clear to me. Tom was the bank robber! Louisa's brother! I was horrified. It would break her heart if he was jailed. And imagine Mr Gradgrind's shame!

The Bad Thing

This is where I have to confess. Where the Bad Thing began. I whispered to Tom, "Escape at once, for your father's sake, and your own!" I told him to go to the circus and ask Mr Sleary to hide him till I came.

Once Mr Gradgrind and Louisa knew the truth, we made our way, separately, to the circus. The idea was to sneak Tom to Liverpool, and then abroad. We said our goodbyes to him, and all seemed set until, without warning, flipping Bitzer appeared.

He'd been sent to fetch Tom back, to face punishment for the robbery. We all thought the game was up, until Mr Sleary offered to take Bitzer and Tom to the station in the carriage. When he rolled his eye at me, I guessed he was up to something! And when he had a quiet word with Tom, I knew for sure!

Sleary tricks Bitzer.

Mr Sleary's plan worked perfectly. As the carriage headed for the station, the trained horse that drew it began to dance. This was a signal to Tom that a pony and trap was coming alongside. Tom leapt up, jumped into it and away they galloped!

Mr Sleary's equally well-

Bitzer faces some Facts about Mr Sleary's dog!

trained dog made sure Bitzer couldn't follow!

Here are some Facts for Bitzer. Dog: clever, trustworthy, faithful, determined, fierce. Bitzer: pasty-faced, sneaky, cold-hearted, smug, creepy.

So Tom escaped! The Gradgrinds said it was all due to me, and were grateful. But I had been brought up to be clean and honest. I knew in my heart I'd helped a criminal to escape – a scheming robber who had caused the horrible death of a good man like Blackpool. That was a Bad Thing. My only excuse was that I did it for the people who took me in and educated me

(well, they tried) – Miss Louisa and Mr Gradgrind.

There it is. I've got it off my chest, and we must all get on with our lives.

My father? I don't hate him for ditching me, but I know for sure he's dead. His dog, Merrylegs, came back to the circus to die. Merrylegs would never have left Dad if he'd been alive.

Louisa? Maybe she'll find her true love and marry again. Maybe not. We'll stay good friends, I'm sure.

And me? I plan to marry and have children – lots of happy children, with heads full of Fancy. And that's a Fact!

Rotten egg: Tom Gradgrind

"I am a donkey – that's what I am. I am as obstinate as one, I am more stupid than one, I get as much pleasure as one, and I should like to kick like one."

Good egg: Mr Sleary

"…a stout man … with one fixed eye and one loose eye, a voice … like the efforts of a broken pair of old bellows, a flabby surface, and a muddled head which was never sober and never drunk…"

Top Facts 7: Crime

Hard Times features a bank robbery – a pretty big crime by anyone's standards. The ordinary Victorian was more likely to be affected by the hundreds of petty crimes which were an everyday part of life. In *Oliver Twist*, Dickens described a man who "...would look constantly round him, for fear of thieves, and would keep slapping all his pockets in turn, to see that he hadn't lost anything..."

Today, when visiting a shopping mall, you might be warned to "Beware of pickpockets". But on the streets of Dickensian London you'd have had to watch out for a lot more than that. Poverty made thousands of poor people, desperate for food for themselves and their families, turn to con-tricks and crime.

Sometimes it was just a question of stretching the truth. Beggars, for instance, sometimes put raw meat on their leg, then bandaged it so the meat showed, like a raw wound. Others would rub a thick layer of soap on their leg and soak it in vinegar. The soap blistered, looking like pus. The beggars hoped people would feel sorry for them and give them more money.

Sometimes the trickery was much worse. Here's a quick quiz about ten criminal types who'd have been pleased to see you if you'd been in London without your wits about you. (The names have been changed to protect the guilty.)

1 Peggy Gumbly lures children off the street, then steals their clothes to sell. She's known as…

a) a stripper
b) a skinner
c) Clothes Peg

2 Joby Ribbitt lurks in inns and alehouses, and empties out drunken customers' pockets. He's known as a…

a) bug hunter
b) pub crawler
c) boozer user

3 Charlie Trott earns his living as a housebreaker. He is a…

a) home wrecker
b) house louse
c) cracksman

4 Fred Mallitt takes a room in an inn, then sneaks into other guests' rooms to rob them. He's known as …

a) a snoozer
b) a sneak snatcher
c) an inn-truder

5 Arthur Brayne passes fake coins. He is a…

a) shoful man
b) funny money man
c) money minter

6 Alf Cobley slips a few knock-out drops into people's drinks, then robs them. He's called a…
a) boozer snoozer
b) napper
c) drummer

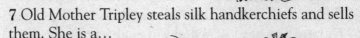

7 Old Mother Tripley steals silk handkerchiefs and sells them. She is a…
a) fogle hunter
b) hanky hunter
c) snifter lifter

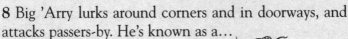

8 Big 'Arry lurks around corners and in doorways, and attacks passers-by. He's known as a…
a) basher
b) bludger
c) nutter

9 Sid "The Snake" Snoak earns his living as a pickpocket. He calls himself a…
a) tweaker
b) buzzer
c) groper

10 Young Joe Betts cheats the public by inviting them to try their luck in a game of dice. Just a gamble, maybe, but these dice are weighted. Joe is a…
a) dicey dealer
b) game boy
c) charley pitcher

Answers:

1b) Peggy watches for a well-dressed child and uses the old trick of offering sweets.

2a) And sometimes he's called a mutcher, or moocher. He's doubly tricky, because he cons a few drinks out of his sozzled victim before clearing out his pockets.

3c) Trott is not your common smash-a-window burglar – he knows all sorts of skilful ways of breaking in.

4a) He might even chat up the guests to find out if they're worth robbing. This low-life will even "work" when he's staying with people he knows.

5a) Arthur is a shoful man, or shoful pitcher. He's at the top of his profession – he makes coins and forges papers, too, such as wills. "Shoful" means worthless stuff, or rubbish. It's not rubbish to Art!

6c) Alf doesn't wait for his victim to get drunk – he helps him along with drugged booze.

7a) She knows the value of a high quality silk hanky, which she calls a fogle. When she can afford to dress better, she'll mingle with well-dressed women and pick better pickings from their pockets.

8b) Big 'Arry, the bludger, uses a bludgeon – a heavy stick or club – to bash his victims.

9b) The Snake is a buzzer, who picks gentlemen's pockets. If he was a wire, he'd pick ladies' pockets. A wire used to hook hankies from pockets with a piece of – guess what? – wire.

10c) Joe's other racket is a game with a pea and three thimbles. He puts the pea under a thimble, shuffles the thimbles about and gets his victim to bet on where the pea is. The victim's always wrong – the pea is jammed under Joe's thumbnail.

Story 6: The Old Curiosity Shop

At number six, *The Old Curiosity Shop* moves between London and the countryside of Victorian England. It centres around Little Nell, who some readers loved, and some loathed. Perhaps they felt she was *too* saintly. Just to even things up, you'll also find one of Dickens's nastiest characters in *The Old Curiosity Shop* – it won't take you long to work out who it is.

The book will make you laugh, shudder, and even – if you're that way inclined – have a good howl. It's a tale of missing persons, vicious bullying, gambling and deception and it all links to Little Nell.

Imagine the tangled web to be unravelled by a Victorian policeman.

The good, the bad, and the extremely ugly

To: **Chief Inspector Medlar**
From: **Constable N. Parker**
Re: **Disappearance of Mr Trent and Miss Nell Trent**

Very complicated case, Guv. Seems to be mixed up with a suspected suicide, and has connections with other recent crimes. I took a number of statements from witnesses.

Case background

Little Nell Trent lived with her grandfather. He was Nell's mother's father, but we don't know his name. Everyone calls him Mr Trent. They lived in the Old Curiosity Shop in London.

They sold all sorts of objects: suits of armour, china figures, wooden carvings, strange furniture – anything curious. Little Nell cared for her grandfather and they seemed very close. Business wasn't brilliant, I gather.

KIT NUBBLES'S STATEMENT

I used to work for Mr Trent. I liked the old geezer, and I just loved Little Nell. She was about 13 when it all started – blue eyes and sweet as honey.

I knew they had money problems, but I never understood why. Mr Trent was worried about what would happen to Little Nell when he kicked the bucket, and he wanted to leave her a nice tidy sum. I also knew that he went out every night, and left the poor girl all alone. I used to stand outside and keep watch whenever I could, but Nell never saw me. Where he went, or what he did, I haven't the foggiest.

Only one person was likely to know a bit about Mr Trent's cash flow, Guv – Daniel Quilp. I got this statement from his wife.

MRS BETSY QUILP'S STATEMENT

I married the vilest, most hideous, horriblest, cruellest man ever. Oh, and ugly – I forgot ugly.

Daniel Quilp had a monstrous head on a nasty little body, with nasty little legs. He had sly black eyes and a grinning mouth with rotting fangs. His hands were rough and dirty with long, yellow nails and he scared me to a jelly. "Yes, Quilp," I'd say, or "No, Quilp," – whichever I thought

The wedding of Betsy and Daniel Quilp.

would keep me out of trouble. "Am I nice to look at?" he'd ask. I'm surprised I wasn't struck down on the spot for the lies I told.

Poor Little Nell. I loved that kiddie, but he hounded her and her grandfather out of their home. Mr Trent used to borrow money from Quilp, you see, and he ended up owing quite a lot. At first, Quilp thought Mr Trent was some sort of miser, stowing the money away somewhere. It's my belief that Quilp would have liked me to drop dead so he could marry Nell and have her fortune. Course it was a different story once he discovered the truth. It seems Mr Trent used to slip out every night, gambling. He gambled everything he had, and kept borrowing more, because he was so desperate to get money for Little Nell. She had a brother, Fred, now I come to think of it.

Next, I went to see a friend of Nell's brother, called Dick Swiveller. He also had designs on Little Nell. I thought he might know a thing or two.

DICK SWIVELLER'S STATEMENT

I'm not a bad sort, you know. I suppose I used to be a bit of a rotten egg when I was younger  – hard-boiled, if you get my drift, old chap. I'm the teensiest bit ashamed of what Nell's brother and I planned. We'd had one or two glasses of the old rosy wine and Fred said he was dead certain that his grandfather had loads of lolly stashed away somewhere. He reckoned it would all be left to Nell. None to him. "You must marry my sister, Nell," is what he said, "then we can share the loot, eh?" Fools, we were. Turned out there wasn't a penny to be had.

Right, Guv. Here's a villain if ever I saw one. Quilp's right-hand-man was Sampson Brass.

SAMPSON BRASS'S STATEMENT

I'm a lawyer. I was a lawyer. I was duped by Quilp. Tricked. Conned.

When Quilp discovered that old Mr Trent was never likely to pay back the money he'd borrowed, he decided to seize the Old Curiosity Shop and sell off the contents. I went along with him. Why shouldn't I? I was his lawyer, and he was a regular client – always needed the law for one thing or another.

We informed Mr Trent of the situation; he knew he didn't have a leg to stand on. However, on the day we went in to seize the property, we found the place unoccupied. They'd gone – the old man and his granddaughter had simply upped and left. Problem solved.

I couldn't help liking young Kit, guv. Read this – you'll see he's a good lad.

KIT NUBBLES'S STATEMENT

It broke my heart when I found out that Little Nell and the old geezer were so afraid of Quilp they'd run away to escape him and that crooked lawyer, Sampson Brass.

Old Trent might have coped with his own ruin, but he couldn't bear Little Nell to suffer. She, bless her, would probably have said something like, "Let us be beggars, and happy." It would have been her idea to take to the road, I bet.

Artist's impression of the missing persons at this time.

I had to take to the road to follow their trail. I tracked down some of the characters they met: Codlin and Short were first. (By the way, Guv, I'll be putting in for expenses — bed and breakfast, ale for these two, etc.

THOMAS CODLIN'S STATEMENT

Travelling Punch and Judy man, I am, officer, sir, with my partner Short. We perform our puppet shows at every village we come across. We're much-loved, we are, and honest as the

day is short – I mean, long. There we were one day, innocently mending our puppets, when Little Nell and old Mr Trent came upon us. Little Nell offered to sew up Judy's skirt. I'm not too hot with a needle and thread, so I said OK. They stayed at the same pub as us and travelled with us next day.

SHORT'S STATEMENT

Soon as we reached the town I blew my trumpet so people would know we were there. We did our show as usual, collected coins from the crowd, then moved on. We all stayed at the Jolly Sandboy that night. If you want my opinion, I don't think the old geezer was quite right in the head. Otherwise what was he doing dragging a poor little girl round the countryside? Worried me,

it did. It seemed to me they might be running away from someone, and I thought it only right to get them to hang around, and then hand them over, like, to their friends.

THOMAS CODLIN'S STATEMENT

Short wanted to tell the Trents' friends where they were. We decided it was best. Short said there might be a reward, but I wasn't thinking of that. Oh no, I was thinking of the poor little girl's welfare, I was.

SHORT'S STATEMENT

Codlin was after a reward for handing them over to their friends, but I only cared about the little girl. As you know, officer, they ran away before we were able to help them. Perhaps there might be a small reward for me thinking of handing them over?

witnesses had some disagreement about events.

I had trouble catching up with the next witness — she moves around a lot.

MRS JARLEY'S STATEMENT

Ooh, yes, dear. They stayed a while with me. Not in one place, you understand. You've heard of me, of course. Mrs Jarley's Waxworks Show is famous the length and breadth of the land, admired by nobility and patronized by royalty. I fed the Trents that night and let them sleep by my fire. They travelled on with me in my caravan. Like to see inside, dear? No? As you like, dear.

Well, that little girl was a treasure. I taught her to lecture. Yes, I said lecture. Her job was to tell the punters – that's the paying customers, dear – all about my waxworks of Queen Elizabeth, or Jasper Packlemerton of atrocious memory. What? Never heard of Jasper Packlemerton? Hand over a few pennies, officer, and you shall see for yourself... Officer? Where are you going?

This bloke's testimony, guv, gives an eye-opener as to how desperate old Trent was to get money for Little Nell.

THE CARD-SHARP'S STATEMENT

Yes, the old man played cards with us. What of it? Not a crime, playing cards, is it? Yes, he lost his money. So what? He got it from his granddaughter, the waxworks girl, so it was his by right, wasn't it? All in the family, like. Never saw them again.

Yes, Guv, he was desperate enough to steal the money from his own flesh and blood. And when he lost it, they were both pretty desperate. They needed a friend, like they'd never needed one before. And that's where the schoolmaster comes into the story.

THE SCHOOLMASTER'S STATEMENT

What an angel! What a child! Dear Little Nell, so good and gentle. I first met her when she and her grandfather stopped me and asked directions. I liked them instantly, and invited them to stay the night. I'd have liked them to stay longer, but they wanted to move on. I begged them not to forget me.

Bless them, they didn't.

It was the strangest thing. Some time later I was walking to my new teaching job when suddenly, bless my soul, there they were – the Trents! Starving hungry, and stony broke.

They needed help badly. The grandfather was exhausted and desperately unhappy. It seems he'd gambled away every penny Little Nell had.

Oh, she was brave. And always cheerful.

It was my joy to help them. I let them use a little cottage, near the church. Little Nell was happy there, but not well. Not well at all.

God bless her.

Course, while the Trents were travelling the country, things were hotting up back in London. Let's go back to Mrs Quilp's statement.

MRS BETSY QUILP'S STATEMENT

We didn't know where poor Little Nell and her grandad were. Quilp offered rewards for finding them. He'd never have paid up, mind you. He also got Dick Swiveller a job at Sampson Brass's. I think he thought Dick could be useful to him, as he was a friend of Nell's brother, Fred.

I was surprised to come across the Single Gentleman (as he's known). He added a new twist to the story.

THE SINGLE GENTLEMAN'S STATEMENT

I heard that my brother – Little Nell's grandfather – was having money problems, so I set about tracing them. I'd made a large

fortune abroad, and I was anxious to help. I lodged at the home of Sampson Brass. Ghastly character, I later discovered.

I met Kit Nubbles, who used to work at the Old Curiosity Shop. Kit heard my relations were with some waxworks show. At last, I thought! A clue! However, Kit was suddenly in appalling trouble.

KIT NUBBLES'S STATEMENT

That git, Brass, lied. He said I stole a fiver, but I never. No one would listen to an ordinary bloke like me, of course. My word against a posh lawyer's? Do me a favour. I got put in the nick.

As you know, Guv, I collared Brass, but you ought to see the end of his statement.

SAMPSON BRASS'S STATEMENT

Quilp made me do it. For heaven's sake, I'm an honest, upright lawyer. I am. Do you seriously believe I would have accused Kit Nubbles of theft unless I'd been forced? I had nothing against the young man, nothing at all. Quilp made me, I tell you. Anyway, you'd never have found out if young Swiveller hadn't been spying on me and tipped you lot off.

Look, I've told you all this of my own free will. We're both men of the law. Put in a word for me, there's a good chap. Reduce the sentence, eh?

In the whole of the Little Nell case, I think Mrs Quilp's statement has the only bit of good news.

MRS BETSY QUILP'S STATEMENT

When Brass got into trouble over Kit Nubbles, Quilp knew the police would be after him. He ran away, as fast as his nasty little legs could carry him, and – now we come to the good bit – he fell in the river and drowned!

I'm free! I'm free!

The Single Gentleman's statement rounded things off.

THE SINGLE GENTLEMAN'S STATEMENT

When Kit was released from prison, we set off and finally tracked down Little Nell and my brother... Eh? Oh, sorry ... where was I?

Tragically, officer, we were just too late. Poor Nell's health had been failing fast. She died. Peacefully, I'm told.

My poor brother was insane with grief, and he died shortly afterwards. We found his body, on a warm spring day, lying on Little Nell's grave.

I'm sorry, officer, there's nothing more I can tell you.

The Single Gentleman is travelling round in the footsteps of his brother and great-niece. He's rewarding those who helped them, and is already reporting back about a number of odd characters he's met. Not all of them are getting a reward, mind. One or two could bear a little investigation them-selves.

All in all, the Single Gentleman may well turn up a good deal more evidence that might explain how those two ended up in such a sorry state.

In my opinion, poor Little Nell died for lots of reasons: her grandfather was stupid about money, Quilp was evil, Brass was crooked, there's not enough kindness in this world for the down and out... I could go on and on, but that's my opinion, if you want it.

I don't.
Signed: Chief Inspector Medlar
(and I'll be checking those expenses)

Dickens data...

The author himself was affected by Little Nell's death. In one letter he wrote, "I am breaking my heart over this story, and cannot bear to finish it," and in another, "I am ... nearly dead with work and grief for the loss of my child."

Rotten egg: Daniel Quilp

"…he ate hard eggs, shell and all, devoured gigantic prawns with the heads and tails on, chewed tobacco … bit his fork and spoon till they bent … in short performed so many horrifying and uncommon acts that the women were nearly frightened out of their wits and began to doubt if he were really a human creature."

Good egg: Little Nell

"If you are sorrowful, let me know why and be sorrowful too; if you waste away and are paler and weaker every day, let me be your nurse and try to comfort you. If you are poor, let us be poor together, but let me be with you, do not let me see such change and not know why, or I shall break my heart and die."

Top Facts 6: That's entertainment

The Victorians didn't have TV, computer games or films to while away their leisure time, but there were plenty of other activities to amuse them. For example, for several years, on Twelfth Night, the Dickens children performed a play in "the smallest theatre in the world" at their home. In *The Old Curiosity Shop* Little Nell came across several entertainers on her travels. Here are some facts about a few more.

1 Theatre
Play-going was a favourite activity during Victorian times, and lots of new theatres were built, some holding as many as 2,000 people. Dickens was a great fan, visiting theatres as often as he could and featuring different sorts of theatrical companies in his novels. Stage versions of his books were put on almost before they were published, and were tremendously popular because they were sure to be packed with high drama and exciting characters.

Many people couldn't read, and this was one way they could enjoy his stories. Dickens was a keen supporter of theatre-for-all; he believed that the ordinary people had, as he wrote, "a right to be amused".

"...the mingled reality and mystery of the whole show ... the poetry, the lights, the music ... the glittering and brilliant scenery, were so dazzling ... that when I came out into the rainy street ... I felt as if I had come from the clouds..."

David Copperfield

2 Music hall

Music hall was a sort of concert, where the audience could drink and smoke (and cough!) as they watched. There might be as many as 50 acts in an evening. The entertainers would sing – opera or comic songs – dance, juggle, perform magic or acrobatic acts, and there was always plenty of comedy, especially slapstick. In fact, the music hall was well known for saucy songs and jokes. Sometimes the audience would become rowdy and throw rotten fruit, but on the whole, music hall was a good night out that wasn't too expensive.

3 Home entertainment

It wasn't possible to go out every night, and many families spent long evenings at home. But the Victorians were clever at amusing themselves. They loved parlour games, playing cards, reading, playing the piano and singing. A guest might bring his own sheets of music, so that he could entertain his host. Some of the sheet music of the times was inspired by Dickens's books. Victorians danced to the "Little Nell Waltz", the "David Copperfield Polka" and "Dora's Waltz" (named after David's wife in *David Copperfield*). They sang the sad ballad of "Poor Jo" (a young crossing-sweeper in *Bleak House*), "God Bless Us Everyone" (Tiny Tim's words in *A Christmas Carol*) and "Walter and Florence", named after the lovers in *Dombey & Son*.

4 Awaydays
Railways suddenly made a day trip to the city possible, or a visit to relations. Fares weren't expensive, so working people could afford to treat themselves to an afternoon at the seaside. Dickens loved the sea, too, and wrote about it in several of his books. Here's how he described it in *Little Dorrit*: "…its thousand sparkling eyes were open, and its whole breadth was in joyful animation, from the cool sand on the beach to the little sails on the horizon, drifting away like autumn-tinted leaves that had drifted from the trees."

5 No beach bums!
If you were transported in your swimming cozzie to a nineteenth century beach, the Victorians would think you were off your head, and you'd be locked up for being almost naked. It was considered improper to show any

part of the body that wasn't normally covered up, and a sun-bronzed skin was only sported by those who worked all day in the open air. A lady remained pale. Men, women and children sat on the beach in their everyday clothes and huge skirts took up a lot of room. Bathing machines were wheeled into the sea. Inside, a lady would change into her swimsuit (long sleeves and legs) and slip into the water without showing even an ankle.

If you didn't want to swim, you could ride a donkey, build sandcastles, paddle, watch a Punch and Judy show, buy a ship in a bottle – even have your fortune told.

6 Street entertainment

Performers did their stuff in the streets – musicians, clowns and acrobats – but there was a nasty side to street entertainment. People bet money on all sorts of things, even rat-killing. Cock-fighting was illegal by 1850, but private fights still took place, with large sums of money being won or lost. The cruel "sport" of bear-baiting was staged in arenas called bear gardens. Savage, trained dogs were set on a chained bear. Bulls were treated in a similar way, and these revolting spectacles continued after they were made illegal in 1835. Some of the heaviest gambling was at prize-fights. These were brutal boxing matches, fought with bare knuckles. Fighters would toughen their fists with pickling solution, and the punching, biting and wrestling would go on until one of the contenders was KO'd, and often badly injured.

7 Horse-racing
Horse-racing meant a good day out for the whole family. Upper, middle and working classes all enjoyed big meetings, such as Derby Day at Epsom. Crowds arrived by train, omnibus, stage coach, carriage and, of course, on foot. It was like being at a fair. Entertainers wandered among the crowds, and there was always someone ready to take a bet from you – or pick your pockets!

"The child … had been thinking how strange it was that horses who were such fine honest creatures should seem to make vagabonds of all the men that drew about them…"
The Old Curiosity Shop

8 Sphairistike, anyone?
Football was a bit rough and ready until the Football Association was formed in 1863 and set rules were agreed on. Professional football was officially recognized by the FA in 1865, and watching matches was a popular Saturday afternoon activity. Little Nell saw "…men and boys … playing at cricket on the green…" much as we might today, but cricket was nothing like the sport we know. Early in

the nineteenth century it was played with curved bats, and bowlers threw underarm until the 1860s, when faster, overarm bowling was allowed. In 1873 a game called sphairistike was invented. Never heard of it? You know it better by its modern name – tennis. And Wimbledon's not so new either. The first world championship was held there in 1877. Tennis was popular and was a game women could play – but only in long skirts!

Day wear

Sports wear

9 Circus

A circus procession was a common street scene, simply because there were many small circuses, moving around from town to town. They were so popular that some cities had a special building for them. London had Astley's Royal Amphitheatre, where trick riders, clowns and acrobats performed in the ring. Dickens had fond memories of visits to Astley's. He wrote: "…there is no place which recalls so strongly our recollections of childhood as Astley's." Much that the Victorians watched would be familiar to us. For instance, Dickens wrote of "the clown making ludicrous grimaces at the riding-master every time his back is turned".

10 Great Exhibition

The Great Exhibition of the Works of Industry of All Nations took place in Hyde Park in 1851. Britain wanted to display her achievements and show the world that British was best. London benefited in a permanent way because profits from the exhibition helped to pay for the Natural History Museum, the Science Museum and the Victoria and Albert Museum. Joseph Paxton, who began his working life as a gardener, designed the stunning, vast building of iron and glass, known as the Crystal Palace. People were afraid it wouldn't be strong enough to stand up, so Paxton had to convince them that his design, based on a lily pad, *was* strong enough. How did he do it? We're told he floated his small daughter on a real lily pad.

Charles Dickens was shown round by Paxton before the building was ready. He didn't like it then, and he didn't like it when the Exhibition opened, either. He had a horror of "sights", he said, and there were far too many sights in one place for his taste. Even the statues of Oliver Twist and Little Nell didn't make him change his mind.

Here are a few more facts about the exhibition:
• Over 6 million people visited the Crystal Palace, among them Queen Victoria, who loved it and went almost every day for weeks and weeks.

117

• The first time many Victorian women used a flushing loo was at the Crystal Palace (but they didn't talk about it). Ladies who were out and about normally had a great problem finding somewhere to go. Even when the Ladies' Lavatory Company opened their first public loos in Oxford Street in 1884, ladies were almost too embarrassed to use them.

• The Crystal Palace measured 563 metres long and 124 metres wide – big enough to contain several football pitches. Paxton built it high enough (33 metres at its highest point) to let three elm trees remain inside – he didn't want to chop them down.

• A major problem was the number of birds getting inside and doing what birds do, especially on ladies' hats. Visitors were not amused. Two birds of prey – sparrowhawks – were brought in to scare off the other birds. Problem solved.

• Thomas Cook, the travel agent, organized special trains to take the public to and from the Exhibition.

There was even a package deal, consisting of train tickets and hotel accommodation in London.

- So the upper and middle classes shouldn't suffer too much from rubbing shoulders with the working classes, the organizers offered five shilling days (25p) and shilling days (5p). The elegant and genteel moved around in comfort on "five bob" days, while the working classes probably had a hot and crowded, but much jollier time for a "bob".

- When the exhibition was over, the building was dismantled and rebuilt in South London, in an area now known as Crystal Palace. It was well known for magnificent firework displays, until it burned down in 1936. (Funny, that.)

Story 5: Great Expectations

If you ever enjoyed rags-to-riches stories like those of Cinderella and Dick Whittington, you'll love Top Ten story number five. It's the tale of Pip, the poor boy whose dream comes true – but that's not all! There's… ROMANCE! Will true love win through? ESCAPED CONVICTS! They'll chill your blood. SECRETS! Everybody seems to have one. LIES! Who can you believe?

Pip's diary over the years must have been a riveting read. If we could look at a few selected pages, what might be revealed…?

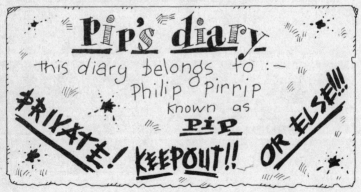

Pip's diary
this diary belongs to :-
Philip Pirrip
known as
PIP
PRIVATE! KEEP OUT!! OR ELSE!!!

My People

Mrs Joe Gargery My bullying sister. She brought me up by hand (and by cane).

Joe Gargery My brother-in-law, a blacksmith with a heart of gold.

Orlick Joe's assistant. Brutal, tries to lick folk into shape.

Miss Havisham Once beautiful, she withered alongside her wedding bouquet.

Estella Pretty proud.

Magwitch A convict who pays his debts.

Compeyson A smooth-talking, cold-hearted criminal.

Biddy My childhood friend. Devoted to me.

Mr Jaggers A lawyer, very sharp.

Pip Me! I wanted to have it all.

Herbert Pocket If you want a good friend, pick a Pocket.

Bentley Drummle Overweight sulky admirer of Estella.

Christmas Eve   ←ME   1843

Cripes! I can't believe today really happened! There I was in the graveyard, looking at my family's gravestone, when this filthy, scary man grabbed me. Legs chained together. Probably escaped from the prison hulk, out on the river. He shook me and licked his lips. "What fat cheeks you got," he said, like he was going to eat me! Told him I lived with my sister, Mrs Joe, wife to Joe Gargery, the blacksmith.

"Blacksmith, eh?" he snarled. He told me to bring food and a file from Joe's forge. "There's a younger man hid with me," he threatened, "who has a secret way of getting at a boy and at his heart and at his liver." I was **SURE** I was going to be eaten. I promised to fetch what he wanted. I've never run so blooming FAST.

Mrs Joe went at me with Tickler, her cane, because I was late. She's 27, twenty years older than me, and she's horrible to me - always "on the rampage" as Joe says. She says if she hadn't brought me up by hand I'd have been in the churchyard long ago.

She means **DEAD**.

I hid some bread, but Mrs Joe thought I'd gobbled it and dosed me with disgusting tar water. YUK. I don't know which is worse – feeling sick or feeling scared. Both about the same I reckon.

<u>Christmas Day</u> – Before dawn, stole cheese, mincemeat and pork pie from pantry. Took brandy from a stone bottle. So Mrs Joe wouldn't notice, topped up the bottle from a jug. Next a file from the forge.

Found the man asleep by a ditch – or so I thought! When he jumped up – it wasn't him! Must have been the one who eats hearts and livers. Ran away, found the right man. Hardly saw the food go, he gobbled so fast. When I said I was glad he enjoyed it, he stared, surprised. Perhaps no one had been kind to him before. Told him about the other man. He nearly went berserk. Left him filing irons off his legs. Don't ever want to see him again.

In the middle of Christmas dinner Mrs Joe offered brandy to her uncle. He sipped, sprang up, spun round, ran to the door and yukked up.

"Tar!" he gasped. I'd filled the brandy bottle with tar water! She looked very suspicious and went to find the pork pie that wasn't there. Oh-oh, I thought, I'm for it now!

SAVED! Just then, soldiers burst in to get Joe to mend some handcuffs. They were after escaped convicts (guess who). Me and Joe followed. The convicts were soon caught. I'm sure my convict recognized me, but before they dragged him away, he said he'd stolen food and a file from the forge. (That got me off the hook.) Kind Joe said he was welcome to it. "We wouldn't have you starved to death, would us, Pip?" he said. When I'm older I'll be Joe's apprentice, and learn to be a blacksmith. He's as strong as Hercules, but kind and gentle. I hope I'll be good like him, not lying and stealing like today. I wish my sister was nicer to him. And to me.

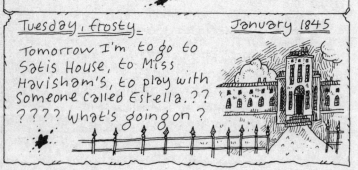

Tuesday, frosty   January 1845

Tomorrow I'm to go to Satis House, to Miss Havisham's, to play with someone called Estella. ?? ???? What's going on?

Wednesday. windy. I hate her. Estella. She's cruel. Miss Havisham's barmy, living in one room in that huge house, wearing a wedding dress. Estella's my age, and pretty but like I said, cruel. She sneered at my clothes, my rough hands, the way I speak, everything. I hate her cos she made me cry. I've got to go back in six days. I won't.

MISS HAVISHAM

ESTELLA

Tuesday. still v. cold   February, 1845

Back to Satis House, but my friend Biddy's helping me with some learning, so I won't look stupid. Miss Havisham's relations were visiting for her birthday. She doesn't like them, and I don't think they like her, though they made out they did. Miss Havisham's got a wedding cake that's all spidery and rotten. Everything's like a dead wedding reception. Ugh. Had to play with Estella again. She's vile to me, but flip, she's pretty. Miss Havisham adopted her. She's going to be educated to become a lady. Wish I was going to be a gentleman, not a blacksmith. Met a pale boy in the garden. Probably one

ABCDE
12+1=13

BIDDY

of the relations. He wanted to
fight, so I did. I beat him, too.
KER-POW!! Afterwards
Estella let me kiss her. Can't
make her out. Girls!

Pale boy

← me now.   Autumn, 1851

Didn't enjoy today. We went to the
Blue Boar to celebrate my being
apprenticed to Joe. He's always talked
of this time, and the fun we'd have
working together. "What larks, Pip!" he'd say.
I'm old enough, now, and strong enough to
start learning to be a blacksmith. Very
odd — Miss Havisham paid my
apprentice fee!

    I've been going regularly to Satis
House for quite a while, wheeling Miss
Havisham round in a chair on
wheels for <u>HOURS</u>. They're posh and
I'm not. Estella won't let me forget
it, either. Embarrassing. Flip,
suppose she saw me at home,
or in the forge. I'd die!

Thursday   Autumn, 1852
    I'm quite experienced at the
forge now — grown stronger as I've
grown older. Yesterday, I asked Joe
for time off so I could visit Miss
Havisham (and Estella). Of course,

126

Orlick — Joe's assistant — wanted time off too. Mrs Joe moaned about it, and Orlick said, "You're a foul shrew, Mother Gargery," (brave or what!) and he and Joe had a set-to. Joe won! **WHAM! BAM!**

Friday = I went to Satis House. What a let-down. Estella's in France for more being-a-lady education. Wished I hadn't gone, especially when I got home and found Mrs Joe had been attacked. Bet Orlick did it! Looks half-dead to me, but Joe says she'll live. Doesn't look as if she'll ever be "on the rampage" again. Biddy's coming here to look after her.

Summer, 1854

Told Biddy I wanted to become a gentleman, so Estella will like me. Biddy tried to warn me off. "I wouldn't, if I were you!" she said. "I don't think it would be the answer." She's sweet — wish I could fall in love with HER, but I can't.

← me (now!)   Early Autumn, 1855

Four years I've been an apprentice, but no more! It's fantastic! My wish is coming true! I'm going to be a

GENTLEMAN! Mr Jaggers, a lawyer, came to tell us someone has given me Great Expectations (money!!), but I'm never to try to find out who. (oh, very difficult. Name beginning with H?) I must buy new clothes and go to London. It's wonderful. So why don't I feel completely happy?

Spring.
1856

I live in London with Herbert Pocket — the pale lad I beat at Satis House! Great fellow. His father educates me to be a gentleman, and I study with Bentley Drummle (arrogant pig — can't stand him). Herbert has gentleman's manners. He said I shouldn't put my knife in my mouth when I eat, and I mustn't stick my fork so far in my mouth. It doesn't half slow you up. I was seven minutes eating my dinner tonight.

Winter
1856

Drizzly and wet.

Joe visited. It was awful. He'd never, ever fit into London society. I knew it. I remember saying to Biddy, "Joe is a dear good fellow... the dearest fellow that ever lived – but he is rather backward in some things. For instance, Biddy, in his learning and his manners." I was right. Today he kept calling me "Sir". I know I'm a gentleman and he's not, but he didn't have to be so stupidly over-polite. I was just plain embarrassed. It all went wrong. As he left, he said, "God bless you, dear old Pip, old chap." and gently touched my forehead. I felt bad then. He was so dignified, in his poor ignorant way. Chased after him, but he'd gone.

The important thing is the message he brought from Miss Havisham. Estella's home and would be glad to see me !!!!! I'm sure Miss H means us to marry !

<u>Winter,</u>
1856

Didn't recognize Estella at first, she's grown so gorgeous — a real lady. She seems nicer, gentler, too. We've both changed. Miss Havisham was weird. She kept on and on saying

"Love her, Pip. Love her, love her, love her!" I do love her, but why Miss H had to make it sound like a curse, I don't know.

Late Winter 1857

A letter from my love! Estella's coming to London and wants me to meet her. I'll take her out to tea.

Thursday   Early Summer 1857

A dreadful shock. A letter came — my sister, poor Mrs Joe, has died. My feelings are so mixed. I remember a time when I was small, and my sister was gentle. Then I remember Tickler and her bad temper.

Started thinking about my own life. Herbert and I have overspent — we're in debt.

Wrote to Joe. Poor Joe — I haven't treated him well. Maybe I'd have been happier if I'd never met Miss Havisham and had stayed a blacksmith's apprentice.

Monday night

Funeral today. Very sad. Promised Biddy I'd visit Joe more often. Could see she didn't believe me. Am I that bad?

me (now!!)

1858

Happy birthday to me, happy birthday to me ... 21 today 21 today ... Jaggers presented me with £500, which I'm to get every year until my benefactor appears. "WOW!", Good old Miss H.! £500 a year and I _KNOW_ she wants me to marry E. Now I can relax and enjoy myself. I also think I might help Herbert get a share in some business or other — in secret. He's such a good fellow.

Autumn, 1858

Weather dull

Fed up. I see Estella all the time but she doesn't love me in the slightest. Today we went to Satis House and she had a filthy row with Miss Havisham. An hour later you'd have thought nothing had happened. Can't make them out.

Spring 1859

Estella _knows_ it makes me miserable when she let's Drummle slobber all over her.

·MISERABLE·

Winter 1860

Strange. I'm 23 now, and STILL Miss Havisham hasn't mentioned she's my benefactor.

Winter 1860

Still wintry. Stormy and wet.

I'm shattered. It's ghastly. After all these years, I discover that Miss Havisham is not my benefactor. It's unbelievable. I have been recieving my good fortune from a convict. An escaped CONVICT. Like a ghost from my childhood, he slunk into my rooms tonight — the very man I stole food for in that churchyard long ago. He's proud that he's made me what I am. "Yes, Pip, dear boy, I've made a gentleman of you," he said. He's asleep in my bedroom. I realize now that, out of pride, I deserted good Joe for a miserable convict who the law says should be hanged.

I feel worthless.

Late Winter
1860

Magwitch, the convict, tells a strange story. The second convict in the churchyard was Compeyson, a "gentleman" crook who was to marry Miss Havisham, but didn't turn up for the wedding. (It must have broken her heart. That's why she kept the house ready for a reception all those years.) Magwitch is in dreadful danger all the time he's here. He'll be hanged if he's caught, so I must get him away from England.

I must also see Estella once more before we leave.

Early Spring 1860

Told Estella I love her. Love her? I wish I could hate her. She has no love for me. She's going to marry that oaf, Bentley Drummle.

<u>Late Spring</u>
<u>1860</u>

My diary's been blank for many weeks — I couldn't hold a pen until today. My hands hurt too much. It's just as painful to remember the night it all happened. Miss Havisham had asked to see me. I told her I was going away. She gazed into the fire and actually said she regrets what she's done to Estella. "I stole her heart away," she said, "and put ice in its place."

It didn't help. I left knowing that Estella's married — and not happily.

Minutes after leaving, just by chance, I looked back. Flames! The house was on fire. I raced inside to get Miss Havisham out, but she ran at me, shrieking, and blazing. <u>She</u> was on fire!

I tried. God knows, I tried. Hopeless. Everything was burning. I couldn't save her.

Now my burns are almost healed, and tomorrow I leave England with Magwitch.

-July, 1860

So much time has passed since that night. Our escape by boat was foiled. Magwitch was captured and sentenced to death. He beat the hangman by dying in prison. I was with him to the end. It's hard to know how I felt, but I do know I truly cared for him.

With Herbert gone abroad (successful businessman now!) I am alone and broke. Had the bright idea of going back to ask Biddy to forgive me and marry me. Fool! With perfect timing I arrived just as she and Joe were celebrating their own wedding. I told her, "You have the best husband in the world."

Tomorrow I leave England to join Herbert and seek my fortune in Egypt.

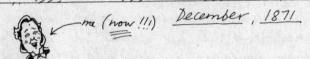

me (now !!!) <u>December, 1871</u>

Eleven years have passed. What a homecoming! Joe and Biddy were thrilled to see me. They have two beautiful children. One is just like me. "We give him the name of Pip for your sake, dear old chap," said Joe, "and we hoped he might grow a little bit like you, and we think he do." I think so too.

Visited Satis House — or what's left of it. Who should be in the garden, but Estella. Her husband is dead. (no loss there — the brute ill-treated her). She asked, "Be as considerate and good to me as you were, and tell me we are friends."

"We are friends," said I.
"And will continue friends apart," said Estella.

I've got plans for far more than that. Great Expectations, in fact!

Rotten egg: Orlick

"He was a broad-shouldered, loose-limbed, swarthy fellow of great strength, never in a hurry, and always slouching. He never even seemed to come to his work on purpose, but would slouch in as if by mere accident..."

Good egg: Biddy

"...her hair always wanted brushing, her hands always wanted washing, and her shoes always wanted mending and pulling up at heel. This description must be received with a week-day limitation. On Sundays she went to church elaborated... She was not beautiful ... but she was pleasant and wholesome and sweet-tempered."

Top Facts 5: Foul London

When Pip was about to go to the city, he said, "While I was scared by the immensity of London, I think I might have had some faint doubts whether it was not rather ugly, crooked, narrow, and dirty." He was right to have doubts. Victorian London was a city with problems. If you took the wrong turning you could leave a tree-lined street of elegant, well-built houses, and stumble upon a rat-infested, stinking slum. If you drank the wrong water it could be the last thing you ever swallowed. Living in London could certainly damage your health. Could you have kept fit and well? Try this quick quiz!

True or False...

1 London rookeries were where flocks of rooks nested, before pigeons moved into the city and took over.

2 There were no cars in Mr Dickens's time, so London was much quieter than it is today.

3 The London air was clean and fresh in Mr Dickens's time, because there were no cars or buses to pollute it.

4 The River Thames was not as clean as it is today.

5 The smell from the Thames forced the government to do something about cleaning up the river.

6 Being exposed to so much dirt and decay meant Londoners became resistant to disease.

7 London might not have been very clean, but if you *did* become ill, you'd be sure of a clean bed in hospital.

8 London's churchyards contributed to pollution.

9 The streets were so dirty that there were crossing sweepers specially to clear a path for people to cross the road.

10 Most Londoners lived in elegant, spacious houses.

Answers:

1 False. A London rookery was a crowded, stinking, squalid area of slum dwellings, such as those in St Giles and Seven Dials. The poor gathered together, like rooks. It wasn't unknown for more than thirty people – not all members of the same family, either – to be occupying just one room. Dickens described: "Ten, twenty, thirty – who can count them! Men, women, children, heaped upon the floor like maggots in a cheese!" Not that everyone was at home at the same time – many would be out begging or stealing, for these districts of poky hovels and twisting alleys, where the sun seldom reached, were ideal places for criminals to disappear from the police. Terrible poverty and appalling living conditions meant poor health for rookery-dwellers, and little hope for the future.

Dickens went into a rookery one night with a police inspector, and described being "…amidst this compound of sickening smells, these heaps of filth, these tumbling houses, with all their vile contents slimily overflowing into the black road…" He peered at crowded sleepers in rooms "…burrowed out like the holes of rats or the nests of insect-vermin."

2 False. In fact, the city was probably noisier than it is now. Barrel organs churned out music, there were coach horns and street entertainers, the rumble of wheels and the clatter of horses' hooves. Above all, there was the noise of the Londoners themselves. Apart from voices shouting, laughing and occasionally screaming, workers had their own particular "cries", such as "Knives to grind!" and "Swe-ee-p!" and "Old chairs to mend!" Dickens described the early-morning racket in Covent Garden: "...men are shouting, carts backing, horses neighing, boys fighting, basket-women talking ... donkeys braying ... and a hundred other sounds..."

3 False. Industries were a major cause of pollution in Dickens's time. Imagine the stink from boiling animal bones to make glue! Or from boiling blood to make manure! Thousands of household fires poured out smoke, and factory chimneys polluted the air with poisonous fumes. London fog turned into dense smog (smelly, smoky fog), making it hard to find your way: "...the fog was heavy and dark... London, with smarting eyes and irritated lungs, was blinking, wheezing and choking..." (*Our Mutual Friend*). Poor visibility made it all too easy to slip up on horse dung or rotting veg, which added to the general stench. Poor drainage, too, ensured a constant pong.

4 True. The River Thames was vile. Sewers emptied straight into the Thames, pouring out household waste (pooh!), dead animals, rotting food, rats. Waste from slaughterhouses (blood, bones and fat) was also washed into the river. The shores were littered with debris, and even the occasional suicide was washed up. When Quilp drowned, in *The Old Curiosity Shop*, Dickens said the river "toyed and sported with its ghastly freight … until, tired of the ugly plaything, it flung it on a swamp … and left it there to bleach."

5 True. The hot summer of 1858 meant that the stink from the river actually stunk out the House of Commons. Surprise, surprise – within a few years London had a new drainage system. Now *that's* what you call a powerful smell!

6 False. As Dickens wrote in *Little Dorrit*: "Through the heart of the town a deadly sewer ebbed and flowed, in the place of a fine

fresh river." Deadly it certainly was. Contaminated water caused many epidemics, and thousands of people used river water for cooking, washing and even drinking. Ignorant of the danger, they took water from parts of the river close to sewer outlets, and water-borne diseases like cholera raged. Victims suffered agonizing stomach pains, vomiting and terrible diarrhoea. Eventually they had trouble breathing and went into a coma. Survival odds were 50:50. Stinking, water-filled ditches ran from the river between rows of houses, and were handy rubbish dumps. People would lower a bucket on a rope to draw up this filthy water, and use it for cooking. In hot summers, children would swim in these putrid ditches, risking cholera and typhoid. Cholera did its ghastly work fairly quickly, but typhoid could be a long drawn-out illness. Sufferers endured weeks of symptoms such as blood poisoning, fever, nosebleeds, bowel trouble, spots, headaches. Eventually the fever would rise and the victim become delirious, with only a one in four chance of survival.

Queen Victoria's husband, Prince Albert, caught typhoid and was ill for weeks before he died in 1861. Victoria never got over it. Her tributes to him include London's Royal Albert Hall and the Albert Memorial.

Because it was easier to get hold of alcohol than pure drinking water, drunks – even tipsy children – were everywhere. In *Oliver Twist*, there were "…little knots of houses, where drunken men and women were positively wallowing in filth…"

7 False. Hospitals were gruesome places early in the century. No attention was paid to cleanliness – bed sheets were rarely changed. Nurses and surgeons, wearing ordinary clothes, treated people without washing their hands. There were no anaesthetics, so patients would do anything to avoid dental or surgical treatment. About 50% of patients were likely to die from shock, gangrene, or new

infections introduced by germ-laden surgical instruments and surgeons' hands. However, in the 1860s, Louis Pasteur proved the existence of microscopic germs, and hygiene began to improve. Sterilization of surgical instruments followed the development of antiseptic surgery, which was pioneered by Joseph Lister with his carbolic spray. Chloroform must have seemed like a miracle when, in 1847, it was used as an anaesthetic. It became quite acceptable to use chloroform in childbirth after Queen Victoria gave it the royal seal of approval.

8 True. London churchyards – what Dickens called "the city of the absent" – became too crowded by the middle of the nineteenth century. Coffins were being crammed one above the other. Sometimes the top one was only half a metre below ground, and the odd bone or skull would work its way to the surface. It was even known for parts of decomposed bodies to wash into the river. In 1855, churchyard burials were stopped and public cemeteries, like the huge one at Brookwood, in Surrey, were developed. Brookwood Cemetery even had a railway station built especially for it, which is still a regular stop today.

(Graveyard legends tell of exploding coffins! It's said that cheapo undertakers didn't embalm bodies properly, and gases built up in the stomachs, causing them to burst. Many tales of graveyard ghosts were supposed to have started with a bang!)

144

9 True. Thousands of vehicles caused a sort of pollution that was very different from London's problems today. Why? Most of those vehicles were pulled by at least one horse! That's a whole heap of manure. Add the general rubbish from millions of people, rotting fruit and veg

from costermongers' carts, dead birds, dogs' mess, and a general slick of dust-enriched mud – and would you want to cross the road in your best shoes? Young children would earn a penny or two from the well-dressed by sweeping a path through the muck. "Dogs, indistinguishable in mire. Horses, scarcely better; splashed to their very blinkers. Foot-passengers ... losing their foothold at street-corners, where tens of thousands of other foot-passengers have been slipping and sliding ... adding new deposits to the crust upon crust of mud..." (*Bleak House*)

10 False. In *Nicholas Nickleby*, Dickens wrote of London, "Life and death went hand in hand; wealth and poverty stood side by side; repletion and starvation laid them down together." The upper and middle classes certainly did live comfortably and elegantly, but it was very different for the poor. Even outside the rookeries, housing could be dreadfully overcrowded. Many properties were rented out by

the room, including the attics and cellars. There are many records of large numbers of people living in one room: for instance, a whole family was found living in a cellar with four pigs. These houses soon fell into disrepair, with crumbling walls and broken doors and windows. They became slums.

A mews was a set of stables, often behind large houses, with living accommodation for coachmen, so they could live alongside their horses. As rich people moved out of London into the leafy suburbs, the very poor took over the mews, and so more slums were created.

Story 4: Oliver Twist

Charles Dickens's second novel, *Oliver Twist,* is probably his best-known story, and it romps in at number four in our Top Ten.

One of his reasons for writing it was to draw attention to the treatment poor people received if they were unlucky enough to be sent to the workhouse. The book tells the tale of a poor boy called Oliver Twist (surprise, surprise) who was born in a workhouse, and who is sucked deep into the criminal world of London.

If the Victorians had had TV, how long would it have been before a boy like Oliver was the tragic subject of a popular TV crime show?

Pete: Good evening, I'm Pete Pryor, and you're watching *Crimes R Us* – our weekly look-at-the-crooks!

Now – a boy is missing, and we want your help. Today, Oliver Twist went to return some goods to a shop. He hasn't been seen since. Reporting a boy missing after just a few hours may seem like overreacting. But in Oliver's case, nothing is as it seems. Our reporter, Suzy Peach, has been looking into Oliver's past. Suzy?

Suzy: Thanks, Pete. The story so far is not a pretty one. Oliver Twist was born and raised in a workhouse. I went to interview the local Beadle…

Suzy: Mr Bumble, tell me about little Oliver.
Bumble: My dear girl –
Suzy: I'm not your dear.
Bumble: Sorry, my d … my goodness, I can't remember

every child who passes through the workhouse. They're all the same.

Suzy: I'm sure you remember this one. You named him, after all.

Bumble: Did I? Perhaps I did. Oh yes, something's coming to me.

Suzy: *(through gritted teeth)* I wish.

Bumble: A small boy. Mother died as soon as he was born. We name our orphans in alphabetical order. T was next, and we were dancing that night. Twist, that's right. Came after Swubble. That's all I remember.

Suzy: Didn't Oliver get into serious trouble once?

Bumble: Trouble? Ha ha. You know lads – always into mischief. Little pickles!

Suzy: Wasn't he locked up, all alone, and beaten every day for a week?

Bumble: No, no, nothing like that ever happens.

Suzy: What do the workhouse children eat?

Bumble: Eh?

Suzy: Eat. You know – food, grub, nosh.

Bumble: They have gruel. Good gruel. Nourishing gruel. The best gruel.

Suzy: And gruel is?

Bumble: Well, I'm no cook … I couldn't say…

Suzy: I'm sure you could. What is gruel?

Bumble: Mmlll worrr.

Suzy: Speak up. Our viewers want to hear. What is gruel?
Bumble: Oatmeal, boiled in water.
Suzy: Oatmeal – boiled in water? That's *it*?
Bumble: It's the very *best* water. Fresh from the river. Most tasty. Oliver loved it. Why, he even asked for more. "Please, sir, I want some more," he said.
Suzy: Oliver didn't love it. He asked for more because he was starving. And for that *crime* he was locked up and beaten. What's more, Mr Bumble, you paid five pounds to have him taken away to work for an undertaker – a coffin-maker! Didn't you?

Bumble: I forget.
Suzy: Mr Bumble, that's all we need to know.

Pete: Ten-year-old Oliver Twist was apprenticed to the coffin-maker, Mr Sowerberry. Neither Mr Sowerberry nor his wife would talk to *Crimes R Us*, but their assistant, Noah Claypole, and their maid, Charlotte, spoke earlier to Suzy…

Noah: Oliver came here and we was all kind to him.
Charlotte: You wasn't.
Noah: Shut up, Charlotte.
Charlotte: Oliver hated it here. The Sowerberries was horrible to him. They only took him cos they got a fiver from Old Bummy, the Beadle, for doing it. They didn't pay Oliver nothing at all.
Noah: Yeah, they was horrible to Oliver, but I wasn't.

Charlotte: You was.

Noah: Shut up, Charlotte.

Charlotte: Noah said nasty things about Oliver's mum, and Olly flipped his lid and they had a good old set-to. Mrs Sowerberry came running, and her and Noah shoved him in the cellar.

Noah: You shoved him in as well.

Charlotte: I never.

Noah: You did.

Charlotte: Shut up, Noah.

Noah: Anyway, Oliver upped and escaped and ran away, and we ain't seen him since.

Pete: The mystery deepened. Nothing was known of Oliver's whereabouts until he was arrested for picking the pocket of a gentleman called Mr Brownlow beside a bookstall.

The truth is that Oliver was wrongly arrested. In court, in front of Mr Fang the magistrate, the terrified child fainted at the thought of the dreadful punishment which awaited him.

RE-ENACTMENT.

The bookstall owner turned up in the nick of time and testified that two other boys were the thieves. Oliver was released, and Mr Brownlow himself took him home and cared for him until today, when he went missing.

That's the story so far. Now, we want your help in identifying the two pickpockets seen that day with Oliver. They may have vital information about where Oliver ended up after running away from the Sowerberries. If we can find that out, it may give an important clue to his present whereabouts.

With the help of the bookstall owner, we've compiled these photo-fits. Who are these boys? Please help.

(*A week later.*)

Pete: Good evening, I'm Pete Pryor, and you're watching *Crimes R Us* – our weekly look-at-the-crooks!

There have been interesting developments in the case of missing boy, Oliver Twist. After last week's programme, we had a call from a woman who recognized the two boys from the photo-fits. She confirmed that they are both thieves, describing them as "a right pair of nickers".

We tracked down the boys, and Suzy Peach spoke to one of them.

Suzy: You're known as the Artful Dodger, and you're a thief and a pickpocket. Is that right?

Dodger: No it ain't.

Suzy: Isn't it true that you met Oliver when he was running away from the Sowerberries and offered him somewhere to stay?

Dodger: Might have. Who wants to know?

Suzy: I do. It was such a kind thing to do for a helpless child.

Dodger: Yeah, well, maybe I did help the little 'un. That's me all over, innit? Kindness itself, I am.

Suzy: Where did you take Oliver?

Dodger: I couldn't say.

Suzy: Why not?

Dodger: I'd get duffed up good and proper if I said.

Suzy: Isn't it true that you took Oliver to stay with a known criminal – a criminal who runs a *school* to train children for a life of crime?

Dodger: Nah – Fagin's a respectable old gent. He don't train kids to steal. He teaches 'em little games to play – they has fun trying to take each other's watches and silk hankies without being spotted. Just stuff like that.

Suzy: Fagin, eh?

Dodger: Oh, heck.

Pete: We're now going live to Suzy who is about to interview Mr Fagin.

Suzy: Mr Fagin. We know you're in there. We want to talk to you about Oliver Twist.

Fagin: Scram. I never heard of Oliver Twist.

Suzy: We understand you train children to pick pockets. Can we come in and take a look?

Fagin: Kiddies? Stealing? I never heard of such a thing. I'm a harmless old gent, I am.

Suzy: But I can see over your shoulder. The place is full of children.

Fagin: What? Oh, them. They're just my little friends that bring me presents now and then.

Suzy: And who is this?

Sikes: My name's Bill Sikes. Who are you, darling?

Suzy: Suzy Peach, reporter for *Crimes R Us.*

Sikes: I'm off. And if you know what's good for you, Snoopy Suzy, you'll do the same. Fagin, keep your gob shut, or you're for a one way trip to the bottom of the river. Come on, Bullseye. We got work to do tonight.

Suzy: I'm coming back to the studio, Pete. Fast.

Pete: There's clearly more to this than meets the eye, viewers. Join us tomorrow evening for *Crimes R Us Update*.

(Next evening.)

Pete: Back to the latest extraordinary developments in the case of Oliver Twist. We're delighted to report that he's been found safe and well, although shaken, at the home of Miss Rose Maylie. Amazingly, Oliver was part of a gang, intent on burgling the Maylie home.

Suzy: You may remember the call from the woman who recognized the photo-fits of the Artful Dodger and his fellow criminal. That woman, Nancy, has revealed much more about Oliver to the Maylie family. It appears that not only is Fagin involved, but Bill Sikes, too. He's the man, you'll remember, who threatened me at the door of Fagin's den of thieves. He's also Nancy's boyfriend.

Pete: Was Sikes responsible for kidnapping Oliver and taking him back to Fagin's clutches?

Suzy: He was, and when he needed someone to help him break into the Maylie house – someone small enough to go through a tiny window – he chose Oliver.

Pete: Oliver is injured, but safe, so we must leave the case to the authorities. We will, of course, keep you informed about any developments.

(Several weeks later.)

Pete: Good evening, and welcome to this special edition of *Crimes R Us* with an exciting update on the Oliver Twist case. We go live now to Suzy Peach in the alleyways of London.

Suzy: The ghastly facts are that Nancy has been battered to death, and her murderer, Bill Sikes, is on the run. We can only guess that she was brutally murdered ... in revenge for her betrayal of Sikes ... who is now cornered at the ... top of a tall ... building ... not far ... from here. There he is!

Suzy: I can't believe it. He's going to leap down and try to swing across a great stinking ditch. He'll never make it! Here he goes! He's slipped! He's falling! He's caught his neck in the rope!

It's ghastly, viewers. His legs are kicking wildly! His body is jerking … dangling … swinging on the end of the rope!

His legs are still now. Bill Sikes has hanged himself.

Pete: A dreadful end for a dreadful man. But what of Fagin, Mr Bumble, Rose Maylie, Noah Claypole and all the other people who played a part in Oliver's life? What of Oliver himself? There are hints that he may even have a half-brother. And who was his mother? Somehow I feel there is a great story to tell…

Rotten egg: Fagin

"Mr Fagin concluded by drawing a rather disagreeable picture of the discomforts of hanging; and, with great friendliness and politeness of manner, expressed his anxious hopes that he might never be obliged to submit Oliver Twist to that unpleasant operation. Little Oliver's blood ran cold…"

Good egg: Oliver Twist

"I will be good indeed; indeed, indeed I will, sir! I am a very little boy, sir; and it is so – so … lonely, sir! So very lonely! … Everybody hates me. Oh! sir, don't, don't pray be cross to me!"

Top Facts 4: The workhouse

In Victorian times, there was no sick pay or unemployment benefit. Those who couldn't work and pay their rent were turfed out on the streets to survive as best they could.

Under the Poor Law of 1834, anyone who needed help had to move into the workhouse. Oliver's mother – cold, pregnant, exhausted, desperate – had no choice but to go there to give birth, and died. The workhouses were run by the parish (a form of local government) and were deliberately made harsh, unpleasant places in order to encourage those who could work to get a job.

So, help for the poorest was available but, as the charitable man in A Christmas Carol said to Scrooge: "Many can't go there, and many would rather die."

Imagine you're a husband and father. You've lost your job, you can't pay the rent, your wife's got nothing to cook, and your children are famished. The only way to survive is for you all to go into the workhouse.

What will your family have to face?

1 You're on your own

Your wife and children will be taken away from you, because men and women live separately. As Dickens sarcastically says in Oliver Twist, "They ... kindly undertook to divorce poor married people ... and, instead of compelling a man to support his family ... took his family away from him, and made him a bachelor!" Don't relax and think the children will be happy with their mother. They'll be taken away from her, too. If you have a boy and a girl, they'll be split up. You'll all be allowed to meet for an hour a week, though.

2 Early to bed, early to rise

Your days will be hard – up at 6 a.m., breakfast over by 7, then work. Your next break will be for lunch at noon, then it's back to work by 1 p.m. Supper is at about 6 p.m. and bedtime is at 8 p.m. That may seem early, but you'll be jolly glad to drop straight off to sleep.

3 Don't talk – eat!

Three meals a day, eh? Sounds good. But meals aren't a right. They're your reward for working hard. You'll sit in

rows at long tables, in silence. You'll probably never feel you have enough to eat, but bear in mind that women get even less than men. You'll mostly have bread, some cheese, and if you're lucky, a little meat twice a week. Is that all? Of course not! There's always gruel. Always. Day after day after day…

"'…don't cry into your gruel; that's a very foolish action, Oliver.' It certainly was, for there was quite enough water in it already."

Oliver Twist

160

4 Lousy haircut

Just so you don't forget where you belong, you'll wear a uniform. You all will. Let's hope you recognize your little girl when you see her for your weekly hour together. Her hair will have been cut short, of course – that's the best way to get rid of lice.

5 No money for old rope

Everybody has to work every day (except Sunday) to earn their bed and board. You didn't think it was free, did you? What sort of work will it be? Could be anything, but one thing's certain – it'll be hard and it'll be boring. Forget all about job satisfaction. You might have to crush animal bones for fertilizer, or smash rocks for roads, or pick oakum. Oakum's a fibre used for stopping up seams in boats, and preventing leaks. Your job is to unravel bits of old rope into strands to be woven together into oakum.

When Dickens visited a workhouse, one spirited inmate "tugged at her oakum as if it were the matron's hair"! You'll soon know how she felt.

6 There's none so blind…

Workhouses are often dirty, overcrowded, and badly run. But then, what's your alternative? Workhouses certainly serve their purpose – they give shelter to those in need. Most of the middle and upper classes have no idea of the awful living conditions of poor people like you. Many close their eyes to what they don't want to see.

161

7 Night noises

Dickens visited the Foul ward of Wapping workhouse in London, and saw that: "Abed in these miserable rooms, here on bedsteads, there on the floor, were women in every stage of distress and disease." There's no privacy in your dormitory. You'll hear every grunt, every snore and every sob from people with no hope of a better life. But none of this will matter much to you. You'll say a prayer for your loved ones, then flake out till morning.

8 Gruel on the grass!

The Poor Law doesn't say anything about workhouse inmates having exercise and fresh air. Your children will lead a dreary, miserable life but if they have a kindly matron she might get the overseer to take them for a walk. They might even be allowed to take their lunch to a local park. *If* they have a kindly matron…

"…he caught sight of Mrs Mann, who … was shaking her fist at him with a furious countenance. He took the hint at once, for the fist had been too often impressed upon his body not to be deeply impressed upon his recollection."

Oliver Twist

9 Don't go, son!

Let's hope your kids don't do what a lot of others do. Some become so desperately unhappy that they run away. They'll have to live on the streets, or in a dangerous, tumbledown building. They'll have to beg or

steal, or make a few pennies sweeping the streets (if they can steal a broom), or hold horses for their owners. Does the thought of your children loose in the city terrify you? Don't worry. Runaways are usually caught – and severely punished.

10 No hope?

Be careful not to get into a fight. It's easily done when so many miserable people live together, but if you do you might be sentenced to hard labour, or even prison. Before you arrived, it's likely you saw the workhouse as the end of the line. You're probably right. There's little hope of you ever getting out. Where would you go? How would you live? Could you desert your family? All you

can do is hope and pray that people like Dickens will speak up for those like you. He wrote *Oliver Twist* to make his readers open their eyes and take a look at the misery just around the corner.

Story 3: A Tale of Two Cities

London and Paris are the cities of the title of our number three story. It takes place against the background of the French Revolution which began in 1789, sixty years before Dickens wrote the book.

France was a land of rich, powerful aristocrats, with titles and great estates, and of poor, downtrodden peasants. Taxes were too high for the peasants, and food prices kept on rising. Eventually the ordinary people couldn't take any more. They revolted.

Dr Guillotin had suggested using a machine for chopping heads off. It was said to be painless, because the falling blade was weighted so heavily that it would slice through the victim's neck quickly and cleanly. It became known as *la guillotine*, and after test runs on dead bodies, it was soon slicing off the heads of live victims, especially blue-blooded aristocrats. Being rich and powerful couldn't save you. Even the king and queen were guillotined.

A Tale of Two Cities, begins a few years before the Revolution…

Heads, You Lose

The Citizens and Aristos.

Lucie Manette, young and lovely (swoons a lot).

Jarvis Lorry a bank clerk.

Ernest Defarge, Parisian wine-seller.

Madame Defarge, Ernest's wife.

Dr Manette, Lucie's dad.

Charles Darnay, French aristocrat real name Charles St Evrémonde.

Barsad, a spy (He'll snoop for anyone if the price is right).

Stryver, a lawyer.

Sydney Carton, does odd jobs for Stryver (spitting image of Darnay).

Marquis St Evrémonde, Darnay's uncle (high and mighty aristo).

Gaspard, a father (but not for long).

Gabelle, the Marquis's official (he's hot stuff).

Lucie Manette meets Mr Lorry of Tellson's Bank, at Dover and learns that her father, Dr Manette, who she thought was dead, is in Paris, alive.

HE WAS IMPRISONED IN THE BASTILLE FOR 18 YEARS. HE'S FREE NOW, STAYING WITH A WINE SELLER CALLED ERNEST DEFARGE. WE MUST GO AND FETCH HIM.

THIS IS SUCH A SHOCK.

FAINT THUMP

In Paris, people are starving, angry with the wealthy aristocrats who don't seem to care. Ernest Defarge gazes out of his wine-shop doorway, grumbling. Mme Defarge knits the names of the aristos who are for the chop when the peasants rise against them.

LOOK AT ZEM, SCRAPPING OVER SCRAPS OF FOOD. ZEY ARE REVOLTING.

BLOOD

ZEY WEEL BE REVOLTING WHEN THE REVOLUTION COMES.

COMTE DE LESS

TELL US YOUR NAME, M'SIEU.

I.M. INNOCENT 105 NORTH TOWER, BASTILLE PRISON.

HELLO, DAD.

Lorry and Lucie find the wine shop. Defarge takes them up to the room where Dr Manette lives and makes shoes. Dr Manette has forgotten his past life, and only remembers his cell in the Bastille.

They return to England. On the rough crossing home with her father, Lucie glimpses an incredibly handsome hunk, Charles Darnay.

MR BARSAD, ISN'T IT TRUE THAT YOU MADE UP THIS STORY TO GET MONEY? THAT YOU'RE DISHONEST, YOU'VE BEEN IN PRISON? THAT YOU'RE A CHEAT AND A LIAR?

Five years later, Charles Darnay is charged with treason and faces execution. The witness, Barsad, says Darnay passed secrets to England's enemies. Mr Stryver, Darnay's lawyer, cross-examines him. The Manettes have returned to France.

NO. HONEST.

Lucie Manette testifies that she saw Darnay on the boat from France, with two Frenchmen. She's upset because she's made things worse for him. Stryver asks his associate, Sydney Carton to step forward.

CRUMBS! I'M AS SOBER AS THE NEXT JUDGE, YET I'M SEEING DOUBLE! IF I CAN'T TELL THEM APART, NO ONE COULD HONESTLY SWEAR DARNAY WAS THE MAN ON THE BOAT. CASE DISMISSED. GO HOME.

NO, GASPARD! ZE POOR CHILD DIED QUICKLY, PAINLESSLY. HE WOULDN'T 'AVE 'AD A 'APPY LIFE ANYWAY WHILE ZE ARISTOS RULE US.

The Marquis tosses the child's father a coin, to make up for the child's death.

OUR FAMILY NAME OF EVRÉMONDE IS DETESTED IN FRANCE. I CAN'T BEAR BEING RICH WHILE SO MANY ARE SO POOR. MY NAME IS NOW DARNAY. I'M LEAVING THE FAMILY, THE MONEY—EVERYTHING—AND GOING TO ENGLAND

SHUT ZE DOOR BEHIND YOU.

At the marquis's grand home, his nephew arrives from England. He is Charles Darnay.

Next Morning...

ZAT EES A NICE WAY TO START ZE DAY. NOT

169

171

172

Three years later, French aristocrats have fled to safety in Britain. Darnay has heard that Gabelle is in prison, and resolves to go to France in secret to save him. He's sure he'll be in no danger, because he's given up the family name and wealth.

YOU KNEW MY WIFE, DEFARGE. WON'T YOU HELP ME?

NOT A CHANCE, MON BRAVE. MY DUTY IS TO MY COUNTRY AND MY PEOPLE.

In Paris, Darnay is identified by Ernest Defarge as "the emigrant Evrémonde" and locked up in La Force prison. The laws have changed since the revolution began, and all those who emigrated from France are to be executed if they return.

Dr Manette, Lucie and Little Lucie hurry to France to try to help Charles Darnay. Dr Manette tries, as the famous "Bastille prisoner," to persuade the citizens of Paris to let Darnay go. He fails, but becomes the prison doctor and sees Charles regularly, which comforts Lucie.

15 months later, Darnay's case comes up.

HIS FATHER-IN-LAW IS ZE GOOD PRISON DOCTOR.

WHY DID YOU COME BACK TO FRANCE DARNAY?

TO SAVE THE LIFE OF CITIZEN GABELLE.

The jury votes to free Darnay. The people cheer and carry him home shoulder-high.

A letter, found in Dr Manette's cell in 105, North Tower, is read to the court. It describes the cruel, chilling treatment of a brother and sister, who died at the hands of members of the Evrémonde family. The dead couple had another sister. Her name is Mme Defarge.

DARNAY, YOU ARE AN EVRÉMONDE. YOU SHOULD DIE!

I QUITE AGREE. HE WILL BE GUILLOTINED TOMORROW.

Sydney Carton carries the distraught Lucie home to Little Lucie.

CARTON, PLEASE SAVE MY PAPA!

I SWORE I WOULD GIVE MY LIFE FOR YOUR HAPPINESS.

Carton tells Mr Lorry to have Lucie and her family waiting in a coach at two o'clock next day. Barsad sneaks Carton into Darnay's cell.

BARSAD! CARRY HIM OUT AS IF HE IS ME. TELL THE GUARDS MONSIEUR CARTON FEELS FAINT WITH EMOTION.

Later that day a coach hurtles towards the coast, and a boat to safety in England.

SYDNEY CARTON KEPT HIS WORD. HE IS TO DIE FOR MY HAPPINESS.

Rotten egg: Barsad

"…the patriot, Barsad, was a hired spy and traitor, an unblushing trafficker in blood, and one of the greatest scoundrels upon earth since accursed Judas – which he certainly did look rather like."

Good egg: Lucie Manette

"If one forlorn wanderer then pacing the dark streets … could have seen the drops of pity kissed away by her husband from the soft blue eyes so loving of that husband, he might have cried to the night … 'God bless her for her sweet compassion!'"

Top Facts 3: Punishment

Britain's prisons topped the European league tables for hellish conditions, so Manette and Darnay were probably better off in French jails. Punishment, to the Victorians, meant punishment – no cushy prison cells with telly and a balanced diet! Some sentences were short and sharp – a few days' hard labour and a whipping was a common punishment – but others meant long terms in prison. And the new police force kept the prisons full. Here are the punishing facts.

1 Bobby job

The Metropolitan Police were created in 1829 by Sir Robert Peel replacing the River Police and the Bow Street Runners. The new policemen were known as "bobbies" and "peelers" after Sir Robert, which was an improvement on the Runners nickname. They used to be called "Robin Redbreasts", because of their scarlet waistcoats. Cute. The Met men had truncheons (called nut-crackers) and a lantern, and wore reinforced top hats. The hat protected their heads and came in handy for standing on to look over walls. These bobbies walked the beat for up to nine hours at a time, and if they needed help, they used a rattle. In later years, they changed to whistles, because rattles couldn't be heard over the racket from traffic. Dickens explored night-time London with Inspector Field, whom he

'ELLO, 'ELLO, 'ELLO!

described as "…vigilant, lamp in hand, throwing monstrous shadows on the walls…"

"The Constables, and the Bow Street men … took up several obviously wrong people, and they ran their heads very hard against wrong ideas, and persisted in trying to fit the circumstances to the ideas, instead of trying to extract ideas from the circumstances…"

Great Expectations

2 Snap those fingers

In the early days of police work, criminal identification was a chancy business. A villain in *David Copperfield* is hunted with the information, "Man to be identified by broad nose, and legs like balustrades of bridge". Sketchy, to say the least! Things did improve, though. After 1880, when it was realized that every fingerprint is unique, Sir Francis Galton worked out a classification system so fingerprints could be identified easily. His system was used as the basis for the modern science of fingerprint identification. Photography, developed in the middle of the nineteenth century, made it possible for the police to keep mug-shot books, like photo albums. Before, they'd had to rely on written records of villains. Criminals were photographed with their hands on their chests, so a man with, for instance, two fingers missing, could be even more easily identified.

Jimmy "Fingers" Fox.

3 Holy terror

Britain's prisons were known to be the worst in Europe. The appalling, filthy conditions were intended to put people off committing crimes, but they were always well-populated. Newgate was particularly dreadful, with dark, chilled cells. Stronger prisoners stole blankets from weak ones, who suffered dreadfully from the cold. Dickens once saw, in the Newgate chapel, a special pew – a black penned area for condemned prisoners. On the Sunday before they were due to die, they sat in this pew and, Dickens said, were made to hear prayers for their own souls and to "join in the responses of their own burial service". This was meant to be a warning to other prisoners to mend their ways. Wandsworth chapel had a different system. All the inmates were put in narrow cubicles, like upright coffins. They were unable to see anyone except the minister, and couldn't see or speak to each other.

PSST... D'YOU EVER GET THAT "BOXED IN" FEELING?

When prisons became overcrowded, old unseaworthy ships were moored near the coast and in the Thames estuary, to house convicts. Magwitch, in *Great Expectations*, has just escaped from one of these hulks when he first meets Pip.

4 Cash dash

A sponging house was a little like an open prison. People who'd got themselves into debt were taken into the sponging house, where an official called a bailiff was the landlord. It was the last chance to sort out their problems before going to prison. When Dickens's dad was taken to a sponging house, young Charles was sent on frantic errands to try to raise some money.

5 Owing, going, gone

Marshalsea prison, in Southwark, housed those who couldn't pay their debts. It was a gloomy barracks of a place, with high, spiked walls. It must have been a lot better than prisons like Newgate, though – it even had a skittle alley. In *Little Dorrit*, Dickens described "the very limited skittle-ground in which the Marshalsea debtors bowled down their troubles". Like Dickens's dad, many prisoners had their families living inside with them, who were allowed to come and go as they pleased.

6 Wheely hard work

In *Oliver Twist*, a man arrested for playing the flute was imprisoned for a month, with the remark that "since he had so much breath to spare, it would be more wholesomely expended on the treadmill than in a musical instrument". Prisoners were sometimes put on the treadmill, which was like walking upstairs for hours on end. The "steps" were fixed to a giant wheel and, by climbing them, the wheel turned. Sometimes it operated pumping or grinding machinery. It was exhausting work, used as a form of exercise or as a punishment.

Other prison jobs were sewing sacks and sandbags, making mops, mats, baskets and brushes, cooking in the prison kitchen or washing in the laundry. It was hard, tedious work.

7 Behave – or else!

The "grind wind", as the treadmill was known, was probably preferable to other prison punishments. Break a rule and you might be flogged, starved or put in solitary. What sort of rule? Talking during "silence", for instance, or being rude, damaging prison property, attacking a warder or – how about this? – playing blind-man's buff! Not the gentle game small children play – in those days "buff" meant to thump the blindfolded player.

8 Doing the barmy

Prisoners sometimes deliberately made themselves ill so they could have a few days break in the prison hospital, or infirmary. Mr Pickwick, in *Pickwick Papers*, visited an infirmary, and found it "…a large, bare, desolate room, with a number of stump bedsteads made of iron". A top trick to get one of these short breaks was to eat soap, which caused diarrhoea and sickness. Bearing in mind that soap was made from animal products, you'd have to be pretty desperate to try this. You could always cut yourself and let the wound get infected. Or you might prefer to "do the barmy" which means to pretend you're mad. Of course, conditions being so unhealthy, and the diet being so bad, there were plenty of genuine illnesses, too. And many, many deaths.

9 The land of Oz

Transportation to Australia was a punishment welcomed by some criminals as an alternative to execution or imprisonment. Young, fit people may have seen it as the chance of a great adventure on the other side of the world. First they had to survive a long sea voyage in appalling conditions, then endure harsh conditions in the penal colony which was to be their new home. They were forbidden ever to return to Britain, under pain of death, like Magwitch.

ARE WE NEARLY THERE YET?

WE'VE NOT LEFT THE DOCKS YET, DUMBO!

10 Hang in there

During Dickens's early childhood, over 150 crimes were punishable by death. When Victoria became queen, she passed a law abolishing the death penalty for minor crimes like stealing. There were still plenty of "topping" crimes, though, and street hangings were a popular entertainment for the public. Dickens wrote of those who went "for the attraction and excitement of the spectacle". He couldn't bear the idea of people having fun watching someone die. In 1849 he went to the hanging of Mr and Mrs Manning, to see the crowd's reaction. The public's behaviour disgusted him. He wrote a letter about it to *The Times* newspaper and worked hard to get the law changed so hangings were carried out behind prison walls. Public executions were finally abolished in 1868, two years before his own death.

185

Story 2: Nicholas Nickleby

When Charles Dickens was small, he heard of a boy who had come home from boarding-school in Yorkshire with a gruesome tale. The boy had had an abscess – a pus-filled swelling – which his schoolmaster had ripped open with an inky pen-knife. (Do *not* try this at home!) Dickens occasionally heard more rumours about Yorkshire boarding-schools and, when he became a writer, he decided to have a look at them for himself.

What Dickens discovered inspired him to write our number two tale, *Nicholas Nickleby*. He wanted the public to know that boys at these grim schools were often terribly ill-treated.

Headmaster Wackford Squeers and Dotheboys Hall are grisly creations, but Dickens warned readers that Squeers and his school weren't nearly so horrifying as the real thing.

Nicholas travelled around a good deal. He and his friends and family couldn't phone each other, but they must have written a lot of letters...

Home and away

Miss La Creevy's
Strand, London

Dear Uncle Ralph,
By now you'll have heard from Mother that our
beloved Father has died. We're broke,

and have left our home and friends
in Devon. Mother, my sister Kate
and I are lodging with Miss La
Creevy, the fairly well-known
miniature painter. (I mean she
paints small pictures. She's quite
normal size really.)

Miss La Creevy

We would be pleased if you'd
help us, and hope to hear from you soon. Kate and
I are willing to work at almost anything.

Your nephew,

Nicholas Nickleby (aged 19)

Mother   *Me*   *Kate*

RALPH NICKLEBY & CO.
GOLDEN SQUARE, LONDON

Dear Sister-in-law,
I'm writing to confirm our meeting yesterday when your son, Nicholas, agreed to accompany me to the Saracen's Head Inn, to meet Mr Wackford Squeers, owner of Dotheboys Hall School in Yorkshire. If Nicholas takes the job Squeers offered – that of assistant master at Dotheboys Hall – I will provide for you and your daughter, Kate.
    Yours truly,

    Ralph Nickleby Esq.

DOTHEBOYS HALL

Dear Charlie,
GUESS where I am! In a coach, galloping north! Strange that two old friends such as you and me may never meet again, but it seems that Yorkshire's where I'm to make my FORTUNE. Uncle Ralph (old skinflint) insists I become assistant schoolmaster at Dotheboys Hall in Yorkshire. I get the distinct impression he wants me out of the way. Wonder why.

Uncle Ralph

Anyway – me! A TEACHER! At 19!

My new boss, Wackford Squeers, has one eye, which works quite well. One side of his face is wrinkled and puckered-up. Highly sinister! His clothes are too small and I won't say any more because he's in the coach beside me.

Wackford Squeers

Dotheboys Hall sounds great. The ad in the paper says the boys get pocket money, and they learn languages, all sorts of maths stuff, writing and everything. The food's unparalleled, it says, so that's OK. Only one strange thing – the boys get no holidays.

Cheers,

Nick

PS I've just remembered another weird thing. Uncle Ralph's clerk, Newman Noggs (who has been MUCH nicer to our family than his boss has) slipped me a letter before the coach left. "Take it. Read it. Nobody knows," he said. It's getting too dark to read now. I'll look at it when I get to Dotheboys Hall.

Newman Noggs

Dotheboys Hall,
Near Greta Bridge, Yorkshire

Dear Kate,
Don't show Mum this letter, whatever you do.
She'd go mad with worry. This place is absolutely
the PITS. It's ghastly. The Squeers family are
vile, there's no other word for it.

It's like they think of the boys as enemies. The
"unparalleled" food is the cheapest and nastiest
imaginable. First thing in the
morning, Mrs Squeers forces a
spoonful of BRIMSTONE
and TREACLE (ugh!) down
the poor kids' throats – the
idea is to put them off eating,
so they'll be even cheaper to
feed. When she's finished
she calls up a little boy and
wipes her hands on his hair!

Mrs Squeers

I've no experience of teaching, but I reckon I
can do far better than Squeers. One of
the boys was cleaning the windows,
and Squeers pretended it was part of
the lesson. "The practical mode of
teaching, Nickleby," he explained. "C-l-
e-a-n, clean, verb active, to make bright.
W-i-n, win, d-e-r, der, winder." His
idea is that when a boy can spell the
word, he goes and does it. Strikes me

he's got as much to learn as the boys.

My dormitory is dirty and crowded. I HATE it. I've never been so miserable. Don't tell Mum.

Lots of love,

Nicholas x x x

PS I got this letter from Newman Noggs. What do you make of it? Has he said anything to you?

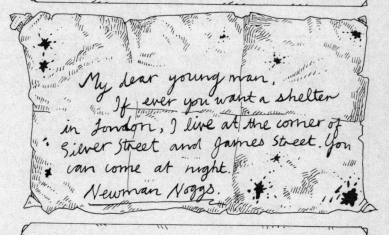

My dear young man,

If ever you want a shelter in London, I live at the corner of Silver Street and James Street. You can come at night.

Newman Noggs.

Dotheboys Hall,
near Greta Bridge, Yorkshire

Dear Kate,

I must tell you about one of the boys, Smike. He's a poor chap, almost my age, who's been here since he was small, but his fees weren't paid after the first

Smike

six years, so he's little more than a slave. He's always wondering if anyone has asked for him (I suppose he means parents) but Squeers always tells him, "Not a word, and never will be."

Poor Smike burst into tears one night, just because I spoke kindly to him. He has no one to care for him — no one at all. He can barely remember the man who brought him here years and years ago. He's so miserable. "No hope, no hope!" he said. "My heart will break. It will, it will." Dear Kate, don't be too upset. I promise I'll be kind to him.

By the way, I've met young Squeers. Master Wackford is a nasty, vicious BRAT. His sister, Fanny, looks very much like her father. Unfortunately, I think she's keen on me. YUK.

Lots of love,

Nicholas xxx

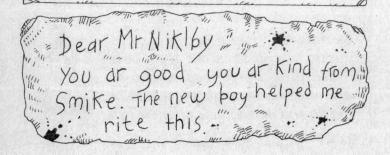

Dear Mr Niklby
You ar good you ar kind from
Smike. The new boy helped me
rite this.

Thames Street, London

Dearest Nicholas,
As you can see, we've moved. Uncle Ralph insisted. Our new rooms are in a dingy old house. Newman Noggs – he's kind – helped us move. It's not bad. Not good, but not bad.

Mama sends her love. I haven't told her anything about Dotheboys Hall because I am absolutely horrified. I wish you could leave at once. But I know you can't, because of Uncle Ralph – honestly, it sounds dreadful. We'll send some food, and you must share it with that poor creature, Smike.

I have some good news! Miss La Creevy wanted to paint my portrait, and while I was posing, I was banging on about not wanting hand-outs from Uncle Ralph, but wanting a job instead. Suddenly, who should arrive, but Uncle Ralph, and he'd found a job for me! Spooky or what!

Madame Mantalini

I work for Madame Mantalini, the milliner and dressmaker, selling her hats and dresses. She's not bad, but Mr Mantalini ... well! Trouble on two legs, he is. He wears the fanciest clothes you've ever seen, dyes his whiskers, and is after all the girls. He flatters Mrs Mantalini, and she falls for it every time. He speaks in the most affected way, and keeps saying "demmit". Not nice.

As I can't show your letters to Mama, will you write her one of her own? And write to me again soon.

Love from your sister,

Mr Mantalini

xxx Kate xxx

Dotheboys Hall,
near Greta Bridge, Yorkshire

Dear Mum,

How are your new rooms? I'm sure you and Kate will make them look lovely. I hope Uncle Ralph isn't being too harsh with you.

I'm fine. Teaching is not a bit like I expected, but Mr Squeers keeps me busy, and I have made a friend called Smike. Don't worry about me. I'm eating properly, I keep myself warm and, before you ask, yes – I'm looking out for a nice girl.

Your loving son,

Nicholas x x x

Dotheboys Hall,
near Greta Bridge, Yorkshire

Dear Charlie,

Girls! I'm sick of girls! I had tea with Fanny Squeers (ugly bug), her friend Tilda (not bad) and Tilda's boyfriend, John Browdie. It was a NIGHTMARE. Can you believe that Tilda and John thought I fancied Fanny? Guess who gave them THAT idea. I'd sooner marry a hippo with warts. Everyone squabbled with everyone else and that was the end of that. Of course, it'll all be made out to be my fault in the end, but who cares?

Cheers,

Nick

Kate, don't write to Dotheboys Hall any more and don't send food. It's all my fault. I spoke to Smike the other night about my leaving, saying something like, "You will do better when I am gone." He asked if he would ever meet me in "the world", as he calls anywhere outside Dotheboys Hall. I promised he would and must have given

195

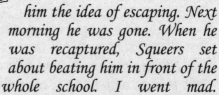

him the idea of escaping. Next morning he was gone. When he was recaptured, Squeers set about beating him in front of the whole school. I went mad. "Wretch," I cried, "touch him at your peril!" I grabbed his cane and, Kate — I thrashed him till he ROARED for mercy. Fanny laid into me, but I was so wild I didn't feel a thing.

Finally I stormed out and will never, NEVER return.

I had hardly any money, but you won't believe who helped me. I met John Browdie and told him what I'd done. "What! Beaten the schoolmaster!" he cried, and was so delighted he gave me some cash to help me get away. I slept in a barn and woke to find poor Smike beside me.

So, we two are homeless, and we're on our way south.

Hope to see you soon, but dare I come home and risk Uncle Ralph finding I've left my job?

Love N

c/o Post Office, Portsmouth

Dear Mr Noggs,

I'm now employed by Mr Vincent Crummles's travelling theatrical company. I'm not boasting, but I've done so well that Mr Crummles just held a benefit performance for me. That means I can keep most of the ticket money.

Mr Vincent Crummles

I'm enclosing a letter and ten pounds. Please give the letter to my mother, and the money to Kate. If you need to, write to me care of the Post Office, Portsmouth.

Yours truly,

Nicholas Nickleby

c/o Post Office, Portsmouth

Dear Mum and Kate,

Sorry I haven't written for ages, but you'll never guess what Smike (he swears he'll never leave me) and I are doing for a living. Get a load of this! We're ACTORS! That's right – actors, on the stage. I've even written a play (well, translated one from French, and everyone says that's the same thing). The manager of the theatre company is Vincent Crummles. He has an amazing daughter, Ninetta. Everyone calls her the Infant Phenomenon because, for someone of her age (she's supposed to be 10), she's amazingly talented. I'm suspicious, though. She's quite short, but her face looks much older than 10, and some of the other actors reckon she's been 10 for at least five years. It's even said that Mr Crummles feeds her gin and water to stop her growth.

I'll send our address as soon as Smike and I settle in one place. I'll be in touch again soon, I promise.

Love from your

Nicholas xxx

CRUMMLES
TRAVELLING THEATRE Co.
will be
APPEARING TWICE NIGHTLY
at a venue near you!
LAUGH, CRY AND BE AMAZED
WATCH THIS SPACE FOR DETAILS

Thames Street, London

Dear Nicholas,

I don't know that acting is a fit profession for a young man but, as you have done so well, I am very proud of you.

I hope you are looking after yourself and Mr Smike. Do eat properly, and wash your ears.

I enclose a letter that arrived for you. The writing is that of a young lady. How exciting! Are we to expect an announcement?

With love from

Mum xx

Dotheboys Hall,
Near Greta Bridge,
Yorkshire

Sir,
I would like you to no that I have written to your unkle to tell him the dreadful things you did to my pa and ma, and how you set about me, a poor defensless young girl. I have no marks on my outside but my insides are damidged, and I am screaming out

loud all the time I write. You
are a monster. I hope your
unkle gets you for what you
did to a ~~mangi magnizif~~ good
teacher and his genteel famly.
                    Yours and cetret
                         Fanny Squeers
PS I will never marry you now, so
          don't arsk.

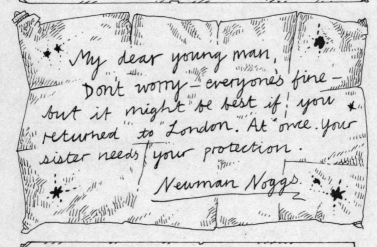

My dear young man,
       Don't worry — everyone's fine —
but it might be best if you
returned to London. At once. Your
sister needs your protection.
                    Newman Noggs.

Dear Mr Crummles,
I'm sorry, but I must leave immediately. I will be
staying with Newman Noggs, corner of James
and Silver Streets, London.
     Thanks for everything.

     Nicholas Nickleby

Miss La Creevy's
Strand, London

To Mr Ralph Nickleby

Sir,
You will note that I have taken my mother and sister back to our former lodgings.

I can't express how disgusted and angry I am with you. You let your vile, boozy friends make rude jokes about Kate, and she's been treated as if she was a cheap, no-good trollop. Sir, my sister is a lady, and don't you forget it.

My family and I want nothing more to do with you. We will make our own way in the world. I shall get a job and support my family myself.

Goodbye.

Nicholas Nickleby

Miss La Creevy's
Strand, London

Dear Mr Crummles,
Sorry Smike and I had to leave like that. My sister was being very badly treated, but it's all

OK now. Smike himself is settled comfortably with us. Mum's kind to him, and it's clear that he likes Kate – a lot.

Say hello to everyone. I miss the stage.
Yours,

Nicholas Nickleby

The Cottage
Bow, London

Dear Charlie,

I've got a proper job! I met two brothers, Charles and Ned Cheeryble. They're amazing. All they want to do is help people, and their business seems to consist of just that – doing good. They've had a clerk for 44 years, Tim Linkinwater. Instead of making him retire (he doesn't want to), they said, "If we could lighten Tim's duties, and prevail upon him to go into the country now and then, old Tim Linkinwater would grow young again." They've given him more time off and employed me to do some of his work. It must be the happiest business in the world.

To cap it all, they've let us have (for no rent at

all) a lovely cottage at Bow. The Cheeryble brothers visit often, and so does their nephew, Frank. Mum thinks he's fallen for Kate. My only worry is Smike. Poor chap doesn't seem too well. Whenever Frank visits, he goes up to his room. Maybe it's too tiring for him when we have visitors. Can't think of any other reason.

Frank

Cheers old mate,

Nick

 PS I've seen the most GORGEOUS girl. Her name is Miss Bray. She's quite hard up, and looks after her father, who seems a ratty, uncaring *Miss Bray* sort. The Cheerybles help her out with money, in secret. Watch this space!

CHEERYBLE BROTHERS
London

Nicholas, old chap. Pop round to Miss Bray, will you, and buy some of her drawings? Be kind to her. She has a rough time, and we care about her a lot. Thanks.

C. Cheeryble

The Cottage
Bow, London

Dear Charlie,

Mr Bray

I had to tell someone! I've spoken to Miss Bray. I ADORE her. Her name is Madeline and she's wonderful. How she came to have such a greedy, selfish father I'll never know. I promised that I will devote myself to her – in fact, I said, "I would die to serve you." And I meant every word.

Cheers,

Nick

PS I fear Smike's health is failing. We were chatting the other day – just about the Cheerybles, how Frank's always popping in, nice things like that, and off he tottered to bed. Mum says he does it every time Frank comes. I did ask if Smike knew what was wrong. "I do; I know I do," he replied. "I will tell you the reason one day, but not now."

The Cottage
Bow, London

Dear Charlie,
I'm bringing Smike down to Devon for some healthy air. He's pretty rough, poor chap. We'll

stay in an old farmhouse not far from you.

The only good news I have is that Frank seems to be in love with Kate.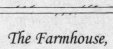

See you soon,

Nick

The Farmhouse,
Devon

Kate, Mum,
Expect me soon, for I am coming home to London. I shall be alone. Our dear friend Smike has died. I am so sad.

With love,

Nicholas x x x

The Cottage,
Bow, London

Charlie,
Sorry to leave without saying goodbye, but I didn't feel like talking. Don't breathe a word of what I tell you. Poor Smike was in love with Kate. I can only think that he wasn't strong

enough to bear the pain of someone else loving her. He took a lock of Kate's hair to his grave. Before he died, he cried out wildly, about seeing the man who first took him to Dotheboys Hall. "I raised my eyes, towards that tree," he said, "and there, with his eyes fixed on me, he stood!"

Charlie, I want to marry Madeline, but strange things are happening. It's all whizzing round in my head and I can't sort it out. There seems to be some sort of connection between Smike and Uncle Ralph. Is it something to do with the man Smike thought he saw?

My darling Madeline has inherited a lot of money that Uncle Ralph tried to fiddle her out of.

Kate and I are in torment. Those we love are rich, and we are poor. How can I propose to Madeline, and how can Kate marry Frank?

You could write a book about my life. What is to become of your friend Nicholas Nickleby?

Rotten egg: Ralph Nickleby

"He knew himself well, and choosing to imagine that all mankind were cast in the same mould, hated them…"

Good egg: Smike

"There was such an obvious fear of giving offence in his manner, and he was such a timid, broken-spirited creature, that Nicholas could not help exclaiming, 'Poor fellow!'"

Top Facts 2: The school story

Of course, not all nineteenth century children attended schools like the ghastly Dotheboys Hall in *Nicholas Nickleby*. In early Victorian times, many poor children had no education at all. But if they did attend school, where would they go … and what was it like…?

1 Those who can, do – those who can't, teach
Dickens wrote, "…any man who had proven his unfitness for any other occupation in life, was free, without examination or qualification, to open a school anywhere…" Halfway through the nineteenth century, there were hundreds of teachers who couldn't even write their own names. (Ask your teacher for her autograph, just to make sure!) Of course, many teachers were excellent but, as the Dickens family proved, anyone could start a school. When money was short, Charles's mum tried to up their income by starting a school at home. Young Charles delivered leaflets to houses near by, telling people about Mrs Dickens's Establishment for Young Ladies. Sadly, nobody came.

NOW CHARLES … ARE YOU QUITE SURE YOU DELIVERED THOSE LEAFLETS?!!

YES!!

2 Bye, kids!
When a widowed mother remarried, her new husband might begrudge having to bring up a couple of small

boys. One way out was to send the kids to one of the notorious (but cheap) Yorkshire schools. These were dodgy places and often little more than prisons. Dickens wrote: "these Yorkshire schoolmasters were the lowest and most rotten round in the whole ladder". One well-known master, William Shaw, advertised a wonderful education, including English, Latin, Greek, writing and arithmetic. The boys would have good food, clothes and anything else they needed, and there would be *no vacations except by the parents' desire*. That meant the children wouldn't bother their stepfather again until they were grown up. What the boys did get was food crawling with maggots, and beds full of fleas. Some of Shaw's pupils went blind because of neglected infections.

3 When you gotta go...

In 1833 the government first dipped its toe into education, and gave £20,000 to charities to help them build new schools. By 1870 the Elementary Education Act said that children aged 5–10 *must* go to school. Education still wasn't free, and many families couldn't afford the couple of pennies it cost each week, so this law wasn't popular with all parents. It wasn't popular with all children, either, and many played truant to work, mind the baby, or just play. By 1891, the fees were abolished and free primary schooling began. Towards the end of Victoria's reign, in 1899, children had to stay at school until 12. (12 years, not 12 o'clock!)

4 There is nothing like a dame
Dame schools were run for small children by women (known as dames) in their own homes. The children were supposed to be taught the beginnings of Reading, wRiting and aRithmetic – the three Rs. These schools were for poorer children, but you still had to pay. Dickens didn't have a good word for dame schools. He heartily disliked the one he'd attended.

5 Sunday school
The Ragged School Union was set up in 1844. These schools gave free classes to those children who were so poor that they would otherwise have no education at all – those who, as Dickens wrote, "are too ragged, wretched, filthy and forlorn, to enter any other place…" They helped children of convicts, tramps and drunks; children who'd run away from the workhouse to live on the streets; orphans and abandoned children; in fact, any needy child. Some children could only go to the Ragged School on Sundays or in the evenings, because they had to work. Apart from the three Rs, pupils were washed and put in clean clothes, they were fed, and they learned work skills, such as sewing, cooking, shoemaking and carpentry.

6 Dance, little lady...

For the rich child, there was a choice. Governesses and tutors could educate them at home. Boys could go away to a great public school, such as Eton, Harrow, Rugby or Winchester. Girls, even rich ones, didn't automatically get as good an education as boys. It was thought more important that they learned embroidery, music, drawing and dancing – subjects they needed for their busy social lives! However, ace schools, such as Queen's College in London, Cheltenham Ladies' College and Manchester High School for Girls brightened the prospects of thousands of girls.

...OUR TOM IS DOING SO WELL AT SCHOOL! HIS MATHS IS MARVELLOUS. HIS LATIN IS EXCELLENT AND AS FOR HIS PHYSICS ...WELL

OH... GOOD! ...OUR ALICE IS A DEVIL AT THE WALTZ!

7 Testing time

Of course, once the government was involved in education, schools had to be inspected. This was nothing like the Ofsted inspection we all know and love. Inspectors toured the schools, testing pupils. This caused a few sweaty brows for the teachers, because they were paid according to results. If a whole class did badly, that teacher would have to go without a few little luxuries. I wonder what an Ofsted team would make of this lesson from *Nicholas Nickleby*:

"'Where's the second boy?'

'Please, sir, he's weeding the garden,' replied a small voice.

'To be sure,' said Squeers… 'So he is. B-o-t, bot, t-i-n, tin, bottin, n-e-y, ney, bottinney, noun substantive, a knowledge of plants. When he has learned that bottinney means a knowledge of plants, he goes and knows 'em. That's our system, Nickleby: what do you think of it?'"

WELL, TO BE HONEST, MR SQUEERS, IT SOUNDS LIKE A RATHER "WEEDY" EXCUSE TO ME!

8 Write right

Clear, elegant copperplate handwriting was taught in schools. It was called copperplate because it was the style used in engravings, and engravings were done on a polished copper plate. You had to have this skill if you hoped to work in an office. Most class work was done by scratching on a wooden-framed slate with a sharp slate pencil. The slate could be wiped and re-used, and we still use the phrase "wipe the slate clean", meaning to forget or forgive and start again. Older children used dip pens and exercise books to practise their handwriting. Apart from the three Rs, there was lots of learning by heart. The Victorian child could recite a great deal of poetry.

"I gazed upon the schoolroom into which he took me… A long room, with three long rows of desks, and six of forms, and bristling all round with pegs for hats and slates. Scraps of old copy-books and exercises litter the dirty floor."

David Copperfield

9 Be good – or else!

Ragged School teachers, in general, tried to keep order using kindness, rather than the cane. It didn't always work. Lord Shaftesbury once found a teacher lying on the floor with six children sitting on him, singing, "Pop goes the weasel". Other schools weren't as soft. There were the "tear-blotted copy-books, canings, rulerings" of the ghastly Salem House in *David Copperfield*. In general, rules abounded and discipline was strict. Bad behaviour or rule-breaking would be punished with the cane or a leather strap. The Victorian child was expected to be obedient, quiet and polite. There were rewards, of course, as well as punishments, and those who behaved perfectly, or whose attendance was excellent, might receive a medal.

10 Tips for survival

Clearly, it paid to toe the line. Here are some tips to stay out of trouble in the Victorian state elementary school.

- Don't talk in class. If you do, you'll wish you'd bitten your tongue off.
- Don't slump in your seat. The teacher will soon make you sit up straight. Whack!

- If you're told to learn something by heart, do it. It's the dunce's cap for you if you don't.
- Don't answer back. The teacher will probably reply with the cane.
- Don't eat in class. The teacher might make you eat something else – like soap.
- Make sure your writing is neat – always. Or you'll be writing line after line after line after line … 100 times.
- Don't be late. You could be kept after school, very late.
- Don't run in the corridors. You'll run the risk of the cane.
- Don't skip school. If you do, the truant officer will bring you in to face the music.
- Mind your Ps and Qs. If you're not polite, you'll be in trouble Pretty Quick.

Story 1: David Copperfield

Here it is! Number one … numero uno … the biggie …
is *David Copperfield*.

"Of all my books, I like this the best," Dickens wrote.
"It will be easily believed that I am a fond parent to
every child of my fancy… But, like many fond parents,
I have in my heart of hearts a favourite child. And his
name is David Copperfield."

It's strange that a brilliant writer such as Charles
Dickens found it so difficult to write about himself. He
did, in fact, write a few scraps of his autobiography, but
eventually gave up and wrote *David Copperfield*. This
story is where we learn about the parts of his childhood
he couldn't talk about. He gives some of these
experiences to the hero, David, then adds a generous
helping of imagination to create an exciting story,
peppered with love, shipwrecks, cruelty, rich men, poor
men, and one of the strangest holiday homes ever.

David had such a colourful life, and met so many vivid
characters, that he's just the sort of person who might be
invited on one of those tell-all TV chat shows…

Micki: Hi, everybody. Let's hear a big warm welcome for – David Copperfield!

David: Hi, Micki.

Micki: David, any idea why you're here?

David: Nope.

Micki: You're here because someone wants to tell you a secret.

David: Wow. I don't know if I like this!

Micki: I hope you do. What do we think, audience? Should we tell him?

Audience: No! Make him wait!

Micki: OK. David, let's look at your life so far. You never knew your father, right?

David: He died before I was born. My mother married again – Edward Murdstone. He and his sister took over our household.

216

Micki: There was someone else in your life, though. Someone called—

David: Peggotty! My nursemaid. She took me to stay with her family on the beach at Yarmouth. It was fantastic – they lived in a big upturned boat. Oh wow! Is it Peggotty who's brought me here?

(Audience wave "No" cards)

Micki: No, not Peggotty. Let's move on. You weren't so hot at your lessons, we've discovered. A bit stroppy and difficult?

David: Rubbish! You've been talking to Murdstone, haven't you? Micki, he beat me. He was cruel. He treated my poor mother dreadfully. Can you wonder I did badly?

Micki: There are two sides to every story, David. Didn't you bite Mr Murdstone?

David: Too right, I did. He was beating me and I was terrified. Didn't do any good, though. He still beat me, then locked me up for five days. He got rid of me, to Salem House School, which was hell. Creakle, the head, was as bad as Murdstone. He made me wear a sign saying: "Take care of him. He bites." Like I was a dog or something.

Member of audience: Didn't you make any friends?

217

David: That was the only good thing about that place. I made two friends. One was Steerforth – it can't be him who wants to tell me a secret. The other was Tommy Traddles – a wonderful chap. He's a barrister now. If he had a secret, he'd have told me!

Micki: Something tragic happened on your birthday, didn't it?

David: Yes. My mother died. (*Stands up*) Murdstone drove her to her grave! Is he here? Tell me he's here, Micki – I'll gouge his secret out of his insides with a meat hook!

Micki: Sit down, David. Murdstone's not here. Carry on with your story.

David: Peggotty was fired, but they let her take me on holiday again. That was so lucky, because Barkis, the cart-driver who took us, fancied Peggotty and eventually they married. We had a wonderful holiday, with Peggotty's brother Daniel, and Daniel's niece Little Em'ly, and her cousin Ham. But it ended and I went home.

Micki: For good?

David: You kidding? They packed me off to work in Murdstone's wine warehouse, washing and labelling wine-bottles.

Member of audience: How old were you?

David: Ten. I was miserable and lonely. Thank heaven for the Micawber family, where I lodged. Mr Micawber was a hoot. Never used five words where fifty would do. He gave me some advice. I can't remember his exact words, but it went something like: "Annual income twenty pounds, annual expenditure nineteen, result happiness. Annual income twenty pounds, annual expenditure twenty-one pounds, result misery." He should have followed his own advice – always in debt, he was. He can't be here, surely?

Micki: No, David. Audience, shall we tease him a bit longer?

Audience: Some "Yes!", some "No!"

David: Rotten lot! Where was I? Oh, yes, the Micawbers pushed off to Plymouth, so I was totally alone. Things got so bad I ran away.

Micki: Home?

David: Not likely. I had just one relative – Aunt Betsey Trotwood, in Dover. She visited Mum on the night I was born, blew her top because I wasn't a girl, and she'd never laid eyes on me since. I decided to go to her. I had to walk, and I arrived filthy and exhausted.

Member of audience: That's 70 miles. You couldn't have walked!

David: I planned to go by coach, but the swine I paid to carry my bags robbed me of everything except the clothes I stood up in. I had to sell some of those to buy food. I was in a hell of a state when I reached Aunt Betsey's. When she realized who I was, she said, "Eh?" and sat flat down on the garden path. Mr Dick, a relative, lived with her – he wasn't too bright, but Aunt Betsey relied on his advice. He suggested I should be washed and put to bed, which suited me fine.

Member of audience: Didn't she tell the Murdstones?
David: Yes. They came to Dover to discuss my future, but Aunt Betsey told them to clear off, and I began a new life with her and Mr Dick. She even sent me to school.
Member of audience: Weren't you terrified, going off to school again?
David: Not this time. Dr Strong's school in Canterbury was brilliant. I lodged with Aunt Betsey's lawyer, Mr Wickfield, and his daughter, Agnes.

Micki: Agnes?

David: Mmm. Agnes.

Micki: Tell us about Agnes.

David: Gentle, sweet, calm – a good friend.

Micki: Is that all?

David: That's all. Where was I? Oh. Yes. Uriah Heep. He was Mr Wickfield's clerk. A vile, fawning hypocrite, who lied and cheated to get power over people and their possessions.

The Micawbers visited Canterbury for a few days. I was thrilled to see them, but not pleased to see Mr Micawber getting friendly with that worm. Heep's nasty secrets were eventually locked up with him, but not before he did a lot of damage. Still, I had other things to think about. When I left school, Aunt Betsey suggested I have a break in Yarmouth while we worked out my future.

Micki: Did you enjoy the holiday?

David: Yes and no. I met up with Steerforth again, so I invited him to go with me.

Micki: That was kind.

David: It was stupid. I've regretted it all my life. Anyway, we visited Peggotty, who was married to Barkis by this time, then went on to Daniel Peggotty's.

Micki: The upturned boat home.

David: That's right. Daniel had a surprise for me. His

niece, Little Em'ly, was engaged to Ham. Trouble was, Steerforth fancied Little Em'ly too. He even bought a boat and named it after her.

The rest of the holiday was great, then I went home and started work for Mr Spenlow, of Spenlow and Jorkins, the London lawyers. My new lodgings were lonely, but Steerforth turned up one night, and we had a few drinks. That made me happy.

Micki: From my information, you weren't just happy, you were totally plastered.

David: Oh. Yes, well, we went to the theatre. I remember seeing Agnes Wickfield in the row in front. Oh, flip. It's coming back to me now. I was… I was…

Micki: Legless.

David: Yeah. Well, booze under the bridge now, isn't it?

Member of audience: Did you see Agnes again?

David: Next day. She was worried because Uriah Heep was working his way into her dad's business, trying to become a partner. I was bothered because I discovered Heep wanted to marry her, but I soon had other things to think about. My boss, Mr Spenlow, invited me home for the weekend, and I met his daughter, Dora. It was love at first sight. I adored Dora. She was … adorable.

Micki: Did love go smoothly after that?

David: Crikey, no. Next thing, Peggotty wrote saying Barkis was seriously ill. I went to Yarmouth, but he died. Everyone was upset, but that was overshadowed when Ham got a goodbye note from his fiancée, Em'ly. She'd run away and gone abroad – with Steerforth. I felt dreadful. After all, it was me who introduced him to the family. Daniel Peggotty nearly went off his head. He made up his mind to follow them, wherever they went in the world, and bring Em'ly back.

Member of audience: What about Dora?

David: Next time I saw her, she was sitting under a lilac tree, with butterflies fluttering round her bonnet. I proposed to her!

Micki: That must have been a romantic moment.

David: You kidding? Her flaming dog barked at me, growled at the flowers I'd brought her, then ripped them up with his teeth. Anyway, Dora was mine! At least, she was mine in secret.

We couldn't tell her dad yet, because I had to get a better job if I was to support a wife.

Member of audience: Your Aunt Betsey had plenty of money. Why did you want more?

David: She lost all her money, every penny. She was ruined. I didn't understand what had gone wrong; it wasn't my business. I started work for my old headmaster, Dr Strong, on the new dictionary he was compiling and, at the same time, taught myself shorthand, so I could become a Parliamentary reporter. Strewth, I worked hard. I had no social life at that time –

oh yes, the Micawbers threw a party. They were off to live in Canterbury, because Mr Micawber was going to work for Uriah Heep. Clot.

Member of audience: Did you tell Dora's dad about your engagement?

David: No. Someone else did, and on one dreadful day, Mr Spenlow told me the whole thing was youthful nonsense and I must forget about it. He must have been pretty uptight because, later that night, he dropped dead. Dora went to live with her aunts.

Micki: What happened?

David: I asked my friend, Agnes, what I should do. She suggested I write to the aunts. They invited me to visit them – I took Traddles, my old school chum, who by then had become a great friend. Good moral support! The aunts said I could visit Dora twice a week. Oh, I loved her so much – mind you, she often behaved like a little kid. I should have realized…

Micki: What?

David: Nothing. I took Agnes to meet Dora. They got on well. Eventually we married, and the problems began. Dora was hopeless. She couldn't manage money, she couldn't manage servants – some days I was amazed she managed to get out of bed. Shopkeepers cheated her … and the dinner parties! Once when Traddles came, the food was so awful we ditched it and ate cold bacon.

Member of audience: With all these problems, did you give a thought to Little Em'ly and the Peggottys?
David: Of course I did. I'm not heartless. I discovered that Steerforth got tired of Em'ly and tried to dump her on his servant. She went bananas and ran away. Steerforth went off sailing round Spain. Mr Peggotty often came to London, between his trips abroad to find her, so I soon told him the latest.
Micki: David, before you go on, tell the audience about your hobby.
David: Hobby? Hobby! Writing is not a hobby! It's my life, and it's flaming hard work.

Micki: I'm sorry. Tell—

David: You don't just write like you start to collect bottle tops, you know – it's a craft, you have to learn it, and practise—

Micki: Hey, hey – calm down. Whose show is this? I've said I'm sorry. Now tell us about your – craft.

David: I started by writing for magazines and, of course, the newspaper, and when I had success with a book, I gave up my reporting job. I was really making it! However, I've found that happiness in one area of your life is often spoilt by sadness in another area, and that's what happened. I'd given up trying to get Dora to organize herself, and decided just to love the dear little thing for what she was. Sadly, the child we expected was still-born, but worse was to follow, because my darling Dora became weak and ill. Seriously ill.

Micki: Were other areas of your life more settled?

David: Not really. Mr Micawber ranted to Traddles and me about Uriah Heep – his employer. He asked for everybody to meet in Canterbury the next week when, he said, he'd expose the ghastly creep, Heep. But meanwhile Little Em'ly made her way back to England and was reunited with Mr Peggotty. He decided to take the family to start a new life in Australia.

Member of audience: Did Heep cop it?

David: Yes. Aunt Betsey, Traddles, Mr Dick and I met Mr Micawber at Wickfield and Heep's offices. Agnes was there with Uriah Heep. Mr Micawber read out, at great length, a list of Heep's fiddles, forgeries and thefts – he'd nearly ruined Wickfield, and all Aunt Betsey's lost money had been taken by him. Traddles forced him to hand over everything and Heep ended up in prison.

Aunt Betsey, bless her, offered the Micawbers a loan. They decided to join the Peggottys and emigrate.
Member of audience: Is Dora better now?
David: Dora died.
Member of audience: I'm sorry.
David: I decided to go abroad, but first I visited Yarmouth. There was a terrific, wild storm that night. In the morning we found a ship wrecked just offshore, with one man left on board. Brave Ham swam out to him with a rope round his waist, but a giant wave smashed into him. Ham never made it. By the time they pulled him in, he was dead.

227

Micki: And the other man?

David: Dead. I still find it hard to believe, but the man on the ship was Steerforth. Ham died for Steerforth – who stole his Little Em'ly.

Member of audience: You'd lost your wife, your friend had caused Ham's death – how did you feel?

David: How do you think? It was the pits. I saw everyone off to Australia, then went abroad and settled in Switzerland.

Member of audience: Were you still writing at this time?

David: Not at first, but Agnes Wickfield's letters bucked me up so much I started writing again, and my books did rather well. I think … I think it was then I realized how much I loved Agnes.

Member of audience: Why didn't you do something about it?

David: It was too late. We were like brother and sister – we could never be lovers.

Micki: After three years, you returned.

David: Yep. Peggotty was now Aunt Betsey's housekeeper, so there was a great reunion at Dover. I asked Aunt Betsey if Agnes had a boyfriend. "Twenty!" she said, and went on to say Agnes had "an attachment", as she called it. Well, I wouldn't interfere in her happiness. Then, one day, Aunt Betsey said Agnes's attachment was definite and she thought there'd be a wedding.

Micki: And?

David: And nothing. That's it. I just hope she'll be happy. She's an angel.

Micki: You're right, David, she is an angel. But she's an angel with a secret. Come in, Agnes Wickfield!

David: Agnes? Agnes!

Micki: Tell him your secret, Agnes.

Agnes: David, my secret is the name of the man I love, the man I've always loved.

David: I don't think I want to hear this.

Audience: Oh yes you do!

Agnes: David, you fool! Can't you guess? It's you! I love you!

Micki: We'll leave David and Agnes alone, folks. They have lots to catch up on, and much more life to live. Perhaps they'll come back on a future show and let us know how they get on. Good luck to them!

Rotten egg: Uriah Heep

"'Be umble, Uriah,' says father to me, 'and you'll get on. It was what was always being dinned into you and me at school; it's what goes down best. Be umble,' says father, 'and you'll do!' And really it ain't done bad!"

Good egg: Dora Spenlow

"She was more than human to me. She was a Fairy, a Sylph, I don't know what she was – anything that no one ever saw, and everything that everybody ever wanted. I was swallowed up in an abyss of love in an instant."

Top Facts 1: Working children

Charles Dickens used his own childhood work experiences as material for *David Copperfield*. Dickens was lucky. The warehouse job he hated so much lasted just a short time, and from then on he had some schooling and did the sort of work he wanted to do.

Other Victorian working children weren't so lucky. Their days were long, hard and often dangerous. Conditions were changing though, slowly, but surely. By 1833, no one under 9 was allowed to work in factories or mills, and those aged 9–13 could only do a 9-hour day. (Only!) Eleven years later, a 6½-hour day was the maximum for 9–13 year olds, and 12 hours for 13–18 year olds. By 1847, no young person under 18 was allowed to work more than 10 hours a day.

It sounded as if things were improving. Hmm… Were they?

1 Danger – kids at work

Victorian factories and mills were noisy, dangerous places. Small children were especially suitable for working around large, violent machinery. They slithered easily under running machines to sweep up bits of cotton that might jam moving parts. One slip could result in terrible injury. Overseers watched that no rules were broken, and made sure the exhausted children didn't fall asleep. Forty winks could earn them a beating. There were fines for being late, or for breaking one of the strict rules, such as "No whistling". Children sometimes lost arms by catching them in machinery, and dreadful accidents happened when worn-out children fell asleep over their machines. The buildings themselves were dangerous places. When one cotton mill collapsed, a newspaper reported that it "…suddenly fell down, burying all the people at work in it".

2 Dark days

In *A Christmas Carol*, Dickens described miners as people who "labour in the bowels of the earth". Until 1842, children as young as 5 or 6 worked in dark, dangerous coal mines. After that, they had to be 10 to go underground. These children only ever saw daylight on Sundays. Some sat alone all day in metre-high tunnels, working as trappers. Their job was to open a door to let coal trucks through. Older ones wore harnesses, and crawled through wet passages, dragging coal containers behind them. They faced deadly danger every minute of the day, and many were killed by explosions, by falling down shafts, and by being run over by coal-wagons. The air was heavy with

coal dust, so suffocation was a real danger. Flooding, when the tunnels filled, meant little children, unable to escape, drowned.

3 Hot and cold

Even away from the big factory areas, there were smaller industries where conditions were hard. For instance, apprentice lace-makers started work as young as 6 or 7. These little girls did long hours, often in poor light. In winter their hands were too cold to sew, and in summer they were too hot and sticky. Constant sewing was hard going. Dickens described Peggotty's forefinger, in *David Copperfield*, as being "…roughened by needlework, like a pocket nutmeg-grater".

4 Fieldwork

Work for country children was hard, but they had fresh air, and woods and streams to play in. They'd work from early morning until dark, weeding fields, helping with the harvest, or picking potatoes and fruit. Sometimes they were human scarecrows – in *The Old Curiosity Shop*, Little Nell saw "…birds in the trees and hedges, and boys in solitary fields, frightening them away with rattles". Children would help look after animals, too. It sounds good but, remember, they had to stay outside all day, *whatever* the weather.

5 Hot work

Chimney sweeps' brushes didn't work in crooked chimneys, so they sent little boys up, inside the chimney, to clear the soot. The boys used elbows and knees to climb, and to stop themselves falling, so their masters rubbed them with strong salt water, by a hot fire, to harden them. Even so, the boys often came down bleeding. They'd be rubbed with salt again, and put back to work. Many little boys died from burns, or suffocated in clouds of soot. If they survived their chimney-climbing days, they usually died of lung disease before too long. In 1840, the use of climbing boys was forbidden, but it went on

WHEN THE BOSS SAID I'D GET TO THE TOP IN THIS PROFESSION I DIDN'T THINK HE MEANT IT LITERALLY !

until 1875, when sweeps had to be licensed. The police then had the power to check they were no longer ill-treating boys.

"Boys is wery obstinit, and wery lazy … there's nothink like a good hot blaze to make 'em come down vith a run. It's humane too … if they've stuck in the chimbley, roasting their feet makes 'em struggle to hextricate theirselves."

Oliver Twist

6 Home help

Many mothers worked at home and, as soon as the children were old enough, they all helped. The work was terribly badly paid. A woman might have to make a

hundred matchboxes for a penny or two, and she'd usually have to provide her own paste. Brushes were often made by home-workers, but fixing bristles into holes made hands sore. Again, earnings were pitifully low – about a penny for a couple of hundred filled holes. Some families took in other peoples' washing, or minded children – anything to boost the family income.

"Her fingers were white and wrinkled with washing, and the soap-suds were yet smoking which she wiped off her arms... 'Mother died...' said the child... 'Then father said I was to be as good a mother to her as I could ... so I worked at home, and did cleaning and nursing and washing...'"

Bleak House

7 Stitched up

A man who brought sewing work to women at home was called a sweater. This was nothing to do with how much he ponged – he was called a sweater because he made his home-workers work so hard that *they* sweated. The pay was rotten, so daughters who were old enough were soon doing their bit to help. To earn enough money to live, they worked long hours, with hardly any rest or exercise. Their eyes suffered through working in dim light at night.

"There was the girls and their mothers a working at their sewing, or their shoe-binding, or their trimming,

235

or their waistcoat-making, day and night and night and day, and not more than able to keep body and soul together after all…"

Little Dorrit

8 Street traders

How did the Victorian city child earn a living on the streets? One might sell matches that she and her mum had made at home by dipping splints of wood in sulphur. Another might sweep crossings, hold horses or run errands. The bootblack would call, "Shine yer boots, sir?" A costermonger's boy would shout to advertise his fruit or veg while his dad pushed the barrow. The butcher's boy would deliver meat from a wooden tray balanced on his shoulder. Sounds OK – as long as it wasn't snowing. And as long as the child wasn't dressed in rags. And as long as he wasn't ill or starving – or both.

9 Shore thing

Dickens wrote, in *Oliver Twist*, of "…ballast-heavers, coal-whippers, brazen women, ragged children, and the raff and refuse of the river…" The slimy banks and muddy shores of the River Thames were hunting grounds for mudlarks. These were scavengers, adult and child, who collected pieces of coal from passing coal-barges, old rope, copper nails from ships, bones, old clothes – anything worth having or selling. Their bodies were caked with mud, and their ragged clothes stiff with it. A more dangerous place to collect was at sewer outlets, where there was always the likelihood of something valuable being washed into the river.

10 Beat this!

Victorian parents who had a few pounds to spare could make sure their little boy had a secure job for seven years. He could become an apprentice, perhaps to a blacksmith, like Pip in *Great Expectations*, or to an undertaker, like Oliver Twist. These jobs were so secure that the child couldn't leave until his time was up unless his master agreed. The good news was that the boy learned a craft which would stand him in good stead all his life. The bad news was that once he was an apprentice, he was stuck with it, even if he hated it, and even if his master beat him – which he was allowed to do!

Epilogue

David Copperfield is fiction. However, all writers use their own experience in their work, in some way, and Dickens revealed a lot about his own life in this, his "favourite child". We must remember that David himself is not Charles (CD ≠ DC), but anyone who reads the book will find that Dickens, through David, reveals a great deal of his own feelings. Here are ten of the ways in which CD *does* = DC.

- David worked in a bottling warehouse, like CD. He was only 10, whereas CD was 12, but the misery he felt was CD's own remembered misery.

- The school Murdstone sent David to is based on CD's memories of Wellington House, where he was sent in 1824. His headmaster, Mr Jones, was a great cane-wielder, like Creakle. CD was lucky, though, as he wasn't a boarder. Day boys weren't beaten much, as they could easily complain to their parents.

- David's friend, Wilkins Micawber, was based on CD's father. Mr Micawber was always short of cash, like John Dickens, and always waiting for something to turn up. He, too, spent time in prison for debt.

DON'T WORRY CHARLES... SOMETHING WILL TURN UP!

... I'LL REMEMBER THAT!

- CD's loneliness in London, when he was living by himself, is reflected in David's own loneliness. When Micawber was imprisoned for debt, his family moved with him and David had to find lodgings of his own.

- In David's passion for Dora, CD revealed his own feelings when, at 18, he fell wildly in love with Maria Beadnell. Her parents didn't approve of CD, and Maria dumped him after about 3 years.

- Little David said that reading was his only comfort. CD had a small collection of books as a child. These he read and reread, feeding his imagination, losing himself in the worlds of *Robinson Crusoe* and *The Arabian Nights* as his own readers would one day lose themselves in his imaginings.

- David, like CD, taught himself shorthand, and found it hard. He spoke of marks like flies' legs, and how the beginning of a cobweb meant "expectation", and of how his "imbecile pencil" staggered about the paper as if it were in a fit!

- CD used his memories of working for a lawyer, and of being a reporter, to add realism to David's experiences.
- Like David, CD lived for a while in Switzerland. He missed London too much to stay for long, though. He wrote that writing without the magic-lantern of the London streets was too difficult.
- David, like CD, became a successful novelist. While we don't have David's novels to read, we're lucky enough to be able, at any time of our lives, to step into the imagination of David's creator – the author of some of the richest stories in the English language … CHARLES DICKENS.

The American poet, Longfellow, wrote: "Dickens was so full of life that it does not seem possible he could die."

While we have his books, he never will.